Reforming Education for the REAL World

George P. Waldheim, Ed.D.

Reforming Education for the Real World

Copyright 2016, Author: Dr. George P. Waldheim, Paradise, California. USA

ISBN: 978-0-9974310-1-8 paperback
ISBN: 978-0-9974310-2-5 hardcover

First Published in the United States in 2016, all rights reserved. No part of this publication may be reproduced distributed in any form or by any means, or stored in a data base or retrieval system, without the prior written permission of the author.
E-mail: towally@comcast.net.

Book and cover design: Debbi Stocco, MyBookDesigner.com

Printed in the United States

This publication is designed to provide information for all concerned people who are committed to significantly improving teaching and learning in schools and colleges. It is published under the expressed understanding that any decisions or actions taken as a result of reading this publication must be based on your personal judgement and will be at your sole risk. The author will not be held responsible for the consequences of any actions and/or decisions taken as a result of any information given or recommendations made.

Dedication

This book is dedicated to helping those students who struggle to learn in the traditional classroom environment and to those teachers, administrators, and all concerned people who are committed to significantly improving teaching and learning in schools and colleges—thus the prescriptive work: *"Reforming Education for The Real World."*

Table of Contents

Dedication..iii
Acknowledgements.......................................vii
Author Biography..ix
Preface...xi
Introduction...1

Chapter 1: Current Teaching and Learning................7
    The Effects...7
    A Thought..15

Chapter 2: Teacher Responsibilities and Accountability...17
    The Need...17
    Developing an Interest to Learn.......................25
    A Thought..28
    Reforms to Teach More Effectively...................28

Chapter 3: Teach To Ensure Learning....................31
    Ensuring Learning......................................31
    A Thought..39
    Reforms to Ensure Learning...........................41

Chapter 4: Teacher Evaluation.............................43
    The Process...43
    A Thought..51
    Reform Teacher Evaluation............................52

Chapter 5: Teacher Contracts.............................53
    Types and Content.....................................53
    A Thought..62
    Reform Teacher Contracts............................63

Chapter 6: Teacher Education.............................65
    Programs and Learning................................65
    Interpreting Student Test Results....................70
    A Thought..74
    Reform Teacher Education............................74

Chapter 7: Gender Bias 77
    Teaching and Gender Bias 77
    A Thought.. 83
    Reforms to Eliminate Gender Bias in Education 84

Chapter 8: Managing Teaching Improvement.................... 85
    The Processes 85
    A Logical Thought 86
    Final Examinations.................................... 87
    Current Faculty Evaluation 89
    Important Concepts 91
    A Thought.. 93
    Reform the Management of Teachers..................... 94

Chapter 9: Ethics and Teaching 97
    Responsibilities 97

Chapter 10: Reforms for Schools and Colleges............... 101
    Reform Current Teaching and Learning................. 101
    Reforms to Teach More Effectively 102
    Reforms to Ensure Learning........................... 103
    Reform Teacher Evaluation 103
    Reform Teacher Contracts 104
    Reform Teacher Education............................. 104
    Reforms to Eliminate Gender Bias in Education 105
    Reform the Management of Teachers.................... 106
    A Final Thought 107

Acknowledgements

I acknowledge that the initial motivation to write this book was generated by the experiences and suggestions relayed to me by so many current and prior students, and teachers. The commonality of both their experiences and mine, coupled with a mutual intent for significant improvement, served as incentive for this "treatise" of reform.

It is without hesitation that I acknowledge the significant support of my wife Carol, and daughters Kate & Marjorie (Marjorie passed away during this writing), and their unending commitment to helping others learn.

Finally, a written response, *"Reforming Education for The Real World,"* to all those who I have encountered who lamented the tribulations of learning and their desire for a better experience.

Thanks to all!

Author Biography

Professional Experience

The author taught and managed in various environments including the military, business and industry, teacher education, and public colleges/universities. The positions included: Sergeant-US Marine Corps Training Command, Co-Owner of a Manufacturing Company in Buffalo NY, Associate Professor at the University of Nebraska-Omaha/Lincoln NE, Professor and Department Chair at California State University-Chico CA, Dean of Business and Technology at College of the Redwoods-Eureka CA, and Dean of the College of Technology at Ferris State University-Big Rapids MI.

Education

Associate Degree from Erie County Technical Institute (currently Erie Community College) Williamsville NY, Bachelor and Master of Science Degrees in Education from Buffalo State College-State University of New York (SUNY)-Buffalo NY, Doctorate in Education from the University at Buffalo (SUNY)-Buffalo NY.

Service and Awards

Rotarian-Eureka CA, President-Small Business Development Center (SBDC) Humboldt and Del Norte Counties-CA, Vice President-CA Community Colleges Association of Occupational Education (CCCAOE) North/Far North Region, Chair-CA North

Coast Articulation Council, Accreditation Reviewer for Northwest Association of Schools and Colleges-Seattle WA.

"Award of Excellence" for outstanding achievement in education, research, and service to students—Halliburton Education Foundation, University of Nebraska. Prior professional memberships: Society of Manufacturing Engineers (SME), Chair-American Society for Engineering Education (ASEE) Midwest Section Engineering Technology Division.

Preface

To: Parents, Students, Educators, Lawmakers, and the General Public.

Why a book on "Reforming Education for The Real World?" We, in the United States, have an obvious problem; our international education ranking as a country is mediocre yet we are the world's leader in manufacturing, military, food production, space exploration, etc. Why did we miss the boat in education? Our high school "dropout" rate is extremely high and reported SAT test scores (college admissions) are inexplicably low. Depending upon where the information comes from, the government or the private sector, the reported current number of high school dropouts in the United States is approximately 3 million plus students per year. This number, actually a slight improvement over previous years, amounts to about *8,300 students dropping out each day.* On top of all this we have the unreported "stay-outs;" those who have gone through the system, survived bad learning experiences, and have vowed to never return unless forced—in many cases a requirement of employment prevails. Their number is indeterminable, but they present a strong force in public discussion concerning their classroom trauma. Put together, dropouts and stay-outs, that's an awful lot of potential learners who have called it quits on the system so many are deceived into believing that it is, the best there is. Have we lost sight of the forest because of the trees? Come on America! We have a real problem in our educational system; Band-Aid improvements such as new programs and more dollars are not improving student learning. We are behind! Therefore, to meet the needs of the "Real World" (*the world we all live in outside of academia*) and position ourselves as the leader in world education, we need to *significantly* reform an educational system that has deftly convinced itself and the public into believing it's functioning in the best interests of all.

Purpose

The purpose of this book is to reform our current educational system and thus improve student learning in the United States. To do this I will first analyze problems that deter students from learning, in many cases regress learning, and then present serious solutions. These solutions are intended to improve teaching and learning and establish an educational system based on accountability and continuous improvement. Logically, improvement cannot begin until we identify the problems, analyze them, make changes, and religiously continue this process. Therefore, in the spirit of the process of improvement I will discuss many educationally controversial and misdirected practices in great length; not as an adversary of, and/or to, my former colleagues. I have met and worked with some of the finest and educationally committed teachers and administrators in our country. Again, this book is only written in the spirit of significantly reforming current educational practices, thus improving student learning in our public schools and colleges.

The final portions of this book will focus on reforming managerial responsibilities. This includes the implementation of procedures necessary to manage and maintain accountability and continuous improvement in teaching. Relative to all of this will be the application of the problem-solving concept that to change something or someone, we have to change ourselves first in order to illicit a responding change. The key is what the current education system will have to change, or in this case "reform," to significantly improve student learning. *That is what this book is all about!*

Introduction

My name is Dr. George P. Waldheim. I spent the first half of my career in private business plant operations, recognizing and solving problems. The second half was in public education, watching problems develop and magnify in a system operationally ill equipped to solve them. Specifically, 18 years in manufacturing, both labor and management, and 22 years in education, both teaching and administration. Educationally, I have an Associate, Bachelor and Master of Science Degrees, and a Doctorate Degree in Education. Professionally, I began teaching in the Military; afterwards teaching and administering a wide variety of classes from Sunday school to two-year College, four-year College, and then the University. Additionally, I received a Halliburton Foundation "Award of Excellence in Education" and also served as a Coordinator of College Admissions, Academic Standards, and Advisement; an

Accreditation Reviewer for a National-Regional Accreditation Commission, a Department Chair responsible for a number of faculty, a College Dean responsible for faculty and programs, and finally a University Dean. Personally, my wife and I have parented two children from kindergarten to college. I know what it is to be a parent concerned about the education of children.

A Real World Comparison

In the Real World: We pay a seller for the product they sell. If their product does not work, we get it repaired/replaced, or get our money back.

In Public Education: We pay a teacher to learn what they teach. If the learning is poor, we are penalized with a low grade and lose our money.

Analysis: Something about this does not make sense! Even the "Elixir Salesperson" of yesteryear got out of town fast after people found out the "elixir" didn't work.

Current Reality

In business, when problems occur with a product, they have to be solved. If you don't solve those problems, your product becomes unmarketable and you lose money. If you lose too much money you go out of business, so the emphasis has to be on solving problems in order to keep the product current, marketable, and to stay in business. In education, when problems occur with our most important product, student learning, the initial thought is to illogically blame it on the consumer, the student; they don't listen, they don't do the work, etc. Then, to add insult to injury, we ignore or do not even attempt any operational/process changes necessary to "fix" the learning problem by alluding to the long standing verbal excuse that, "we have no control over what the student does." Then again the process is repeated all over with a new class or semester. Little, if any, thought or change is given to resolving the problem of low student learning, except to issue poor grades. Unfortunately, the public educational institution does not go out of business when the product depreciates. Thus, the problems only magnify themselves as time goes on and the result is that student learning potentially decreases because of us, not in spite of us.

Therefore, the sole purpose of this book is to expose the problems I have witnessed and recommend the changes, more so the reforms, necessary to resolve those problems and make us the world's leader in education. To accomplish this will require implementing education process control *(accountability and continuous improvement)* with the overall goal of significantly increasing student learning and reducing our dropout rate closer to a lower structural level; that is students moving in and out of the system due to family/personal relocation versus our current disaster.

I have witnessed the difference between students dropping out of school or being a success in school is, more often than not, directly related to the teaching/learning system. Their decision, to stay or leave, is based on what they experienced. Simply put, with good experiences they tend to stay, with too many bad experiences they go! Good, coupled with bad, students *"learn"* to tolerate poor teaching and discouragement in order to graduate. Rest assured improvement in education is not a one-shot solution, or specifically, more money related. It is a notorious accountability deficiency issue and improvement will require changes in areas that are traditionally "difficult" (taboo) to discuss. It will take many process changes to improve, but collectively it will redirect a system that admittedly can never be perfect, but can and will be one of the best in the world.

A THOUGHT

Teachers, over the years, who have grown to be known as "problematic," such that their poor reputation precedes them, have little influence over their classroom environment because they are deficient. In practice, in our public education system, they are not accountable or answerable for their major job responsibility of student learning and thus lack effective review and improvement. This situation not only facilitates, but perpetuates, poor classroom learning. Unfortunately, those faculty who are deficient, mainly due to the absence of accountability, are in essence—protectively employed. To remedy the detrimental effects of this protection will require a reformation effort sponsored by all the parties reading this book: parents, students, educators, lawmakers, and the general public. Be aware that the parents and students are the front line paying consumers and seemingly not only have a purchaser's right of inquiry about the educational product, but a subsequent and logical obligation to hold their school board, administrators, and faculty accountable for their performance.

As an example, when we purchase food *all* the measurable

INTRODUCTION

product ingredients and performance level of the product (calories) are lawfully revealed for our protection. Purchase education and all the measurable course ingredients (topic objectives) and performance level of the teacher are non-existent. *It makes sense the educational consumer needs all the measurable course ingredients and the teacher's performance level for their decision-making protection.* This will only occur when parents, students, educators, lawmakers, and the general public demand it!

Specifically: *What do we need? Why don't we have it? and, How do we get it? Read On!*

Chapter 1: Current Teaching and Learning

The Effects

If the student doesn't learn, don't be so quick to blame the student! My experience has been, most students who initially enter a class have the mental disposition to want to complete and/or do well in the class. Those who enter a class with a preconceived notion of difficulty or failure have already contracted the notion from previous bad learning experiences that have happened in our system. Thus, I believe it is our responsibility to "repair;" however instead of working to repair and restore those relationships, we justify their future difficulty or failure by relating to their documented past performance. Therefore, it is not our fault. So, we advise them to go somewhere else or give them their well-deserved "F." This "kick the can down the road" solution to the problem tends to get worse and results in greater student alienation of the system: more dropouts and more stay-outs!

As a Dean at a community college, I have interviewed an overwhelming number of students who expressed similar experiences. First, they did poorly in high school because it was just not interesting, didn't make sense, and "they did not learn well." Additionally, the teacher ignored them and gave the attention to the better learners. Thus, they developed a poor perception of themselves; some to the point they remembered being told, "It's too bad you can't learn." Now, later in life, they realize, mostly because of success in their job, they can learn and they come back to school in spite of the prior damage inflicted. Unfortunately, I have seen almost as much damage done in the educational system as success. This is the direct result of poor teaching. Had the teacher been directly responsible for what the students should have learned, the problem being exposed by low test scores (measured course objectives), and given other necessary changes in the system that I will discuss later, those problems would have been prevented from repeating themselves. However, situations like this persist, magnify, and go on year after year. When I continued to interview the returning students, the same names of the teachers inflicting the damage re-occurred, in fact they are probably still doing the same thing today.

I actually meet many older adults who still have nightmares about a class, or classes, they took 20, 30, to even 40 or 50 years ago. When asked, "Was it interesting, make sense, give you the feeling of accomplishing learning that will help you?" They laughed and said, "Just the opposite!" For too many students our educational system did more damage than good. The community college enrollments are filled with students whose prior education experience (elementary and high school) was much less than satisfactory. Thank goodness for the community college system.

It is apparent we have to change what we are doing if we want to become the world's leader in education. Specifically, we have to change/improve the level of student learning, which logically means we have to change the way we teach! Note: In the classroom, we only have a teacher and the students. Theoretically, if we take away the teacher then no learning occurs. Therefore, the teacher, when teaching, causes learning to take place. *The level of this learning can and should be documented; it is the baseline for instructional improvement.* Learning happens in an environment of varying applications of student abilities, interests, dispositions, feelings, etc., much of which is in reaction to the teaching. If we improve teaching, we improve student learning and the student perception/value of learning. Only then will we be able to reduce the dropout and stay-out rates, and be able to reform an educational system currently focused on everything except student learning.

Be aware that today's teaching is too significantly based on what I characterize as "preaching" (expounding, urging—lecture). To the counter-argument "not necessarily so because we use computers," I have to reply No! Computers did not change the preach-teach methodology. By that I mean students *read* the computer screen, on which they are seeing words/numbers etc., and then go about repeating it to themselves as if they heard it from the preacher's mouth; thus the students are preaching to themselves. *Logically, computer programs designed more for "visual learning," rather than the aforementioned preach-teach (verbal learning), will increase by demand when education implements accountability and continuous improvement as described later in this text.*

Now, how effective is the "preach-teach" method? Look at your own life situations. As a parent: "I told them not to do it but they just don't listen." As a friend: "I warned him/her but they just didn't listen." As a whatever, you get the point! Isn't the way information is sent, received, and **learned** dramatically different today than it was verbally 30, 20, or even 5 years ago? If so, why haven't we dramatically changed the way we teach? Teaching by preaching is so ineffective and has persisted too long in schools. Mainly because the educational system's evolution of contractual and legal roadblocks protects this ineffective teaching methodology by preventing administration (management) from making the operational improvement and/or staffing changes necessary, even when justified by obvious and documented "poor student learning."

Do you want to know whom the better, not necessarily the most effective, teachers are? Just ask the students! They know because they are the products we are producing. They have the real experience of what is being learned and at what level. We, for the most part, do not! I remember seeing an institution's school bookstore that had its glass windows completely covered with each faculty member's previous class student evaluation summary page. The students would read the scores and make decisions on what classes to take, based on the scores. Now, how long do you think the posting of teacher evaluations lasted? The next semester all evaluation summaries were removed and thus the problems hidden. I can hear the teacher arguments now, but in reality *the public is paying for learning* and logically has an invested right to see what they get for their money. Unfortunately we are still teaching the same way as hundreds of years ago but then the teachers/lecturers would walk down an aisle and the students would put teaching payment money in the frock-tail rear pouch of their lecture robe. The teacher/lecturer would be paid according to their performance. Next time you go to a graduation ceremony look closely at the frock-tail of the faculty robes that are suspended from the around their necks. You will see the characteristic rear pouch, most likely now a ceremonial dress tradition. Makes you well aware that years ago, teachers were held accountable because payment was directly related to their performance; that is, how the students perceived their *learning:* was it worth it or not? Yet today, in reverse, the student's learning is held accountable by critical ranges of grades and the teacher receives pay regardless of their performance. That certainly does not promote teaching motivation, and in actuality, deters it. I believe this whole reversal in roles occurred because teachers are employed and paid by protective entities such as a town, city, state, etc. rather than directly by the students. Therefore, accountability was shifted to the students and deftly evolved away from the teacher. This misdirected reversal in accountability has spread unquestioned with corresponding detrimental effects on student learning!

So now, where are we with our current teaching and learning? We are in, and have been in, a system that is not able to respond to measured student learning. In fact, as I will outline in the following chapters, our system hides the problems and even promotes the extension of them. We have to reform our system to first evaluate at what level the students have learned the class material, and second, if the learning is low or unacceptable, make immediate changes to the teaching process in order to improve it. The important point will be the level of student learning considered acceptable; not grades on any curve, but a straightforward score and documentation of what the student has learned in the class versus what the student was supposed to have learned in that class. *All subjects included!* Actually, many occupational educators have been doing that for years. Dental, medical, and other technology programs have measurable objectives and standards that must be demonstrated by testing in order for the student to continue in the program. Unfortunately, real faculty accountability for what *all* the students should have learned is not part of the teaching employment system. The current system, because of "preach teaching" (expounding, urging—lecture) caters to only those learners who more naturally absorb enough information from the preaching to pass informational tests on the preaching and move on in the system. This selective teaching practice (preaching) is deceptively justified by the use of statistical sampling whereby the student's grades are analyzed on a graphically shaped curve (example: graphically plotting test letter grades versus number of students attaining those grades). The deception is the inference drawn from the grades: the high grades are inferred to represent high student effort/learning and the low grades just the opposite. *In reality, the grades more logically represent the varying strengths of individual students' modes of learning: hearing, seeing, feeling.* Those few whose natural receptive learning mode for preaching (hearing) is very strong will tend to be at the positive tail of the curve (high grades) whereas those few with very poor receptivity to preaching will tend to be at the negative tail of the curve (low grades). The larger remaining group (varying and less biased modes of learning) appear in the center top and both descending sides of a resultant bell shaped curve. In reality, this deceptive process of grade interpretation appears to justify low grades by relating them to low effort/learning; thus the failure of those who do not learn well from "preaching!" Which, as described before, *is an awful lot of people!*

Important: When a teacher plans and teaches using all the learning receptivity modes: hearing (preaching), seeing (visual), and feeling (application), of their students, with the intent that they all must learn; the results destroy the aforementioned curve, the grading inferences, and the justification for selective teaching by preaching. It is teaching directed to all students, by utilizing all the learning receptivity modes to acquire knowledge. The only variables remaining are the differences in the individual levels of information retention; *they all were able to receive and process the information*, but retained it at different levels. Logically the graded scores would be higher because more students receive the information; thus—**more learn easier!**

Case in point: I once had an administrator review my class grade sheet at the end of the semester and he asked why I had no failures, with the expectation that I should have had some. I told him the way I taught was to ensure all students learned the information at an acceptable level, as documented by measured course objectives, and thus no failures! I destroyed the curve by teaching to each student's mode of learning, ensuring their receptivity of the required subject matter and that was reflected in the testing and subsequent grades. He did not question my answer but I could tell that he was disturbed by it and that only reinforces my argument as to the accepted regimentation of a system that is ill equipped to accept the notion that the only failure in the classroom is the teacher. Please remember, curve reported learning all goes back to the current teaching method which is most generally "preaching." In actuality, the students are being graded on only how well they adapted to the preaching and those that do not are eliminated from the system by low grades, dropping out, or staying out! If the whole notion of preach teaching today is questionable, remember "I told him/her not to do it but they just didn't listen," then what about the evaluation stemming from that, and the advisement, and so on?

Years later those eliminated from the system tend to come back and do very well, some in the same classrooms, and the rhetoric/justification is they are more "mature now." More accurately they were disinterested because of deficient teaching (not on their wavelength); resultantly the topics did not make sense, they didn't understand/retain it, and because of all that they were perceived as poor students. So, where do we go from here? In the following chapters I will examine the changes we need to make in order to reform our system and make us a world leader in education. These changes will no doubt be seen as an attack on the current status quo and be rebuffed by those unwilling to come out of their protective systems. When a student leaves school, they find out real quick in most jobs in our society you either perform or leave. Why should teachers employed with the responsibility of student learning be any different? Teaching resulting in poor student learning and performance cannot be tolerated in an educational system accountable to the public that pays the bills and the teacher's salaries. It is time to stop listening to excuses, start making the changes to reform and build a system based on documented student learning as the main objective. **How? Read on!**

CHAPTER 1: CURRENT TEACHING AND LEARNING

A THOUGHT

To teach to all students, utilizing all three modes of learning receptivity, requires necessary pre-preparation by the teacher. Because of a deficient lack of teacher accountability, this pre-planning *rarely occurs* and the cover-up practice is to assign student homework - *conceptually in error!* In reality, the homework is nothing more than the same "preaching" (students reading to themselves) mode of learning, emphasizing the deceptive practice that more preaching is better *for all*. This practice is only positive reinforcement to those biased towards the hearing mode of receptivity but *conceptually in error* by actually promoting negative learning reinforcement to those more receptive to the visual and feeling modes. Because the homework is not on their "wavelength" (even more difficult to learn at home than in class) those not as receptive to preaching struggle and become *much more* discouraged and disinterested, thus they dropout or survive with low grades and become a stay-out. This is where the teacher "fails" the student. I do not mean by giving them an "F," although that may be a consequence of such deceptive and deficient teaching. *Teaching incorporating all three modes of learning for all course objectives must be a religious part of classroom instruction and is the teacher's "homework" responsibility.*

Think about this: An obvious fact is those stay-outs who learned to survive in the current system, in spite of the aforementioned deficient teaching, have displayed and proven an exceptionally strong commitment to "want to learn." Who is the real failure in their classroom?

Reform Current Teaching and Learning

- Teachers and administrators must directly accept responsibility and accountability (be answerable) for student learning.
- Limit selective teaching by "preaching" (expounding, urging—lecture).
- Teach by ethically utilizing all three modes of learning receptivity for all course objectives.
- Develop student interest in all the subjects taught in the classroom.
- Promote student accomplishment for all students in the classroom.
- Measure, grade, and analyze student learning thus documenting teacher effectiveness.

Chapter 2: Teacher Responsibilities and Accountability

The Need

It is a misleading statement to say the foremost responsibility of a teacher is to teach. Unfortunately, in daily usage, the verb "teach" has become more a figure of speech used to represent too many differing perceptions, camouflaging the teaching profession from its foremost responsibility. Theoretically, one can teach and give instruction but that in no way assures learning; this is the problem we face in our nation's educational system. So, how do we define the verb "teach?" Dictionary examples include "to impart knowledge," "to bestow," "to give instruction," or more specifically, "to cause to learn." I believe the real message, in the definition of the verb "teach," is that something happens because of it! We are imparting, bestowing, giving, etc. *Well, how well are we imparting, bestowing, giving, etc., or how well are students learning?* What is the ultimate logical outcome of the process of teaching? It must be "student learning!" That is the very reason we are teaching; so students learn. Now, one can teach until the equator freezes over but if the students do not learn the teaching effort is in vain. To be clearer: *The teacher's responsibility is, and has to be, "student learning."* End of story!

Now, what does the teacher have to do to promote and ensure "student learning?" To start, we have to ask and answer the question: Student learning of what? A necessary part of ensuring learning is all major topics of instruction, therein to be learned, should be documented by learning objectives and a corresponding method of measuring student accomplishment of those objectives. Note: For the purpose of this discussion, the word "objective" is a noun and refers to that which is created by the teacher, and then is worked for to achieve. The definition of the word "goal" is for defining the overall purpose of a course of instruction. In essence, the overall course will have a goal, and subsequent to that, the informational topics necessary to reach that goal will be made up of cumulative measurable objectives.

Measurable objectives? How can one tell if the learners have met the topic objectives if they cannot be measured or if the objectives just plain do not exist? If learner accomplishment of individual topic objectives cannot be measured, then we cannot document if learning of those objectives actually took place, at what level, and the effectiveness of the teaching. *Whatever material is being taught, it should be derived, planned, and implemented with measurable objectives and the subsequent evaluation results analyzed to document the effectiveness of the teaching and the teacher.* Yes, some courses and/or subjects currently have measurable objectives in place, but unfortunately too many do not!

To those critics who say, "Where have you been?" I say:

Let's see the level of effectiveness of a teacher at your institution documented by a class grade average based on a comprehensive final examination or cumulative tests, grading all course objectives; all students—no exemptions.

Let's see a comparison of the teachers at your institution relative to their effectiveness as documented by a class grade average based on...

Let's see your institution's published minimum acceptable level of teacher effectiveness relative to student learning as documented by a class grade average based on...

I can hear the screams of privacy already, "Yes you are paying me, but my level of performance is confidential!" Come on! I can even find out the effectiveness rating of a product on "Amazon.com" before I purchase it. Here in public education, for the most part, after the class is paid for and over, it is hidden. Makes you wonder why, doesn't it?

Now, think of this: If the class comprehensive final examination grades, for all the students in the class, show half of the class received grades of C and above, and the other half received grades of C and below, that would indicate a lower level of student learning versus a similar class showing C's and above. This process would reveal the level of learning that took place, relative to the course objectives, and thus the effectiveness of the teaching.

We have to ask the question: What is the minimum acceptable level of teacher effectiveness for a class, relative to documented student learning, at your school/institution? Not sure? Educational institutions are always concerned about student learning but when it is tied to teacher effectiveness they act immune and unknowing! Without documenting the effectiveness of teaching, there can be little accountability to the teacher's job responsibility of "student learning." Little accountability breeds little improvement and/or complacency; this is the situation we are currently in. *If we want to improve education, we have to document how effective our teachers currently are, specifically based on documented student learning, and then analyze and implement a continuous process of improvement.* We must be able to show where we currently are, and then, where we are going. Doing this we improve! Not doing this we regress!

Getting back to course objectives: For the most part math, science, and occupational related courses appear to be somewhat compliant; probably due to certification, registration, or other institutional, commercial, or standardized testing requirements. These entities, for the most part, require documentation of a student's performance. My personal experience during institutional accreditation review is that courses and the instructional material related do identify a course goal and then define *minimal* general objectives to meet that goal. Examples of student performance (generalized testing) are usually provided to the reviewer with other course related materials, many times voluminous. *Please note:* I have reviewed numerous individual instructional course materials as a Regional Accreditation Reviewer, Faculty Member, Department Chair, College Dean, and University Dean. *In most cases, cumulative topical measurable objectives for the entire course and corresponding methods of documenting student performance of those objectives did/does not exist.* Usually, just a couple of course cover sheets indicating the goal of the course and a few stated objectives relative to that goal, including a grading system for the course and other class information relating to attendance, assignments, etc. In the minimal of cases where strong documentation existed concerning cumulative topical objectives and performance assessment of those objectives, they were presented mostly by teachers who had significant experience in business, health, technologies, or other world of work occupations before teaching.

The problem in education is that we do not have or promote this "assurance of performance," for both teacher and student, other than a final course grade which in too many instances is derived from data far removed from actual measurable performance of course objectives. Think about it, if the teacher presents a topic and then assesses the learning of that topic, the outcome of the assessment not only documents student learning, but also and more importantly, the effectiveness of the teaching. At that point, the teacher could/should determine what changes have to be made to increase student learning for that topical objective. The changes could include re-teaching the topic, changing the presentation methodology, etc. The important part being, the teacher now knows how effective their teaching was and now has the opportunity to determine what changes they have to make, if necessary, to assure an acceptable or increased level of student learning. Unfortunately testing is viewed as a threat by students and is generally ignored by teachers as an assessment of a teacher's effectiveness. The very nature and culture of this philosophy has to be changed in order to increase and assure student learning.

It is a teacher's responsibility to clearly design, draft, and document all course major topics with written measurable objectives. Complimentary, the teacher must develop and document objective ways to measure the student performance of those topic objectives. This is not an easy task and I believe it is avoided because of the work involved. Unfortunately, too many current teachers take the easy way out, and leave this task to the writers of related course texts and test questions at the end of the textbook chapters. This is a good example of what not to do! Textbooks are written in specific readable format and are a good tool to accompany a teacher's informational format but are not, and should not, be the course inclusive. To do this is to lose the advantage of individualized instruction; related material developed and presented in a multi-mode format by a teacher who is familiar with the varying learning characteristics of the students in the class. The course topic objectives and the methods to teach and measure the accomplishment of those objectives should relate to the specific student group, in a person-to-person class setting.

Note that some state and national "standardized testing" requirements may persuade teachers to identify measureable objectives for all the major topics being taught in their course. This probably would occur out of a teacher's necessity to respond to whatever results are identified by standardized testing. If standardized test scores are low, the institution response may be "poor student performance" whereas the student/parent response may be "poor teaching." In either case, the learning level of the students and the effectiveness of the teaching can and should be revealed by evaluating individual course objectives versus their corresponding class examination

Chapter 2: Teacher Responsibilities and Accountability

grades. This review would identify what and where the problems exist and serve to justify resolution. If this documentation does not exist then the "disease cannot be identified and/or treated" and the patient (the student) permanently suffers (grades on transcripts do not disappear), and the problem only tends to repeat itself with a new group of students. On the other hand, high standardized test scores can be reviewed back to identify student and teacher performance, and the results used to promote even better teaching.

I realize the critics of standardized testing are strongly commenting that high standardized test scores relate to the teacher teaching the test. However, it is logically accepted that standardized tests are derived from numerous individual topic objectives for the given course as identified by some outside agency: federal, state, county, etc. Actually, when you think about it, the people designing the standardized tests are identifying individual course objectives from which to formulate the standardized test. They, in fact, are doing the job the teacher should be, or should have done prior to the course being taught. Then, they are assessing student performance of those objectives just as the teacher would, or should, be doing. Had this process occurred in individual classes or courses then there would not be such a strong need for standardized testing except for academic comparisons on larger scales. Additionally, the importance of standardized testing serves to not only identify student achievement, but also document teacher performance. Unfortunately, as outlined in other chapters of this text, the resolution of poor teacher performance under the current administrative and management systems needs to be overhauled because it generally cannot be an immediate fix. Without an immediate fix the problem procrastinates and infects a completely new class by repeating itself.

Now a controversial topic: For a teacher who does not identify and teach using topical objectives and document student achievement of those objectives, then "teaching the test" may be an alternative. At least the topics deemed important by more than one person, as in public education, would be identified and taught with accompanied documented learning. If we, as a nation, want to be a leader in world education then we have to promote excellent teaching, discourage poor teaching, and prove it! Standardized testing is only a threat to those who are poor teachers. Remember, the only failure in the "real world" classroom is the teacher! If learning does not take place, then the "cause to learn" has been ineffective and that is one of the primary job responsibilities of the teacher. This can only be resolved through documentation and resultant change.

On the issue of standardized testing: One must agree there are certain subjects/courses that relate to most curriculums of study and are natural candidates for standardized testing. Therefore it seems reasonable for educational systems to maintain similar course content in math, science, language, etc. Even the Greeks agreed on their "trivium" of lower division subjects (grammar, rhetoric, logic) thus demonstrating their educational common agreement. We cannot ignore that as geographically widespread an educational system that we have, and as competitive as the educational systems have become, there should be some commonality in courses; thus the outcomes of those common courses would necessitate documented accountability.

Chapter 2: Teacher Responsibilities and Accountability

Developing an Interest to Learn

What does the teacher have to do to promote student learning? In addition to documenting the learning objectives for individual courses, and the method of student measurement for documenting and analyzing the learning of those objectives, it is a fundamental responsibility of the teacher to generate the "cause to learn." Necessity is the mother of invention; without establishing and convincing students of the necessity of learning the individual objectives it will be that much more difficult for learning to take place. People do what they tend to be interested in; if the teacher does not or cannot develop student interest in the subject matter of the topic objectives, one cannot expect students to learn just because they are told about it, or told to do it. This is one of the greatest challenges the teacher faces: determining how the individual course topic objectives meaningfully relate to the students. If a student is convinced the information presented is needed, then real learning tends to take place. If the student cannot see the need or necessity in the information, they either memorize it or just plain let it go out of the memory window. Overall, I believe it has long been accepted there is a strong correlation between interest and learning. The teacher must develop "necessity interest" in the student if formidable learning is to take place.

How many of us have sat in classes at either the elementary, secondary (high school), or college level and wondered why we were even there. Unfortunately, some whole courses are this way and they persist semester after semester. Years later, generally in the world of work, some significant happening will trigger the memory flash of that boring teacher and class with the wonderment of why the teacher did not use what just happened as an example to generate interest. Too little class preparation, too late, too little experience, or possibly the teacher just preached and was not really interested in "student learning." This type of teaching is what we have to prevent if we want to be the world's leader in education. I have witnessed new teachers, those just entering the profession, tend to take more time to investigate interests and motivate their students even though they may not have significant experience in the course material. They are extremely interested in what they are doing and the impact they will make. Additionally, those new teachers, who have spent a number of years in the world of work before beginning the profession of teaching, have the advantage of experiencing real life applications of the course material and find it easier to promote student interest; convincing others of why it is important! Those professional teachers in the middle group seem to be split into two groups. Those that can create such student interest you can hear a pin drop in their class. I have actually witnessed experienced "general education" teachers like this who, on occasion, had extra UN-enrolled students sitting in the aisle space of their classroom just to see, feel, and hear the topical information with their class enrolled friends because it was presented multi-mode, and thus so interesting. Then, the other type of teacher, who was just doing enough of their job to escape the wrath of a litany of complaints. All of the above situations would be clearly exposed, good or bad, by measuring student performance of all course topic objectives to determine the level of student learning and the effectiveness of the teaching. This could then be reviewed by the faculty member and supervising administrator at the end of each course of instruction and appropriate "continuous improvement" plans and actions taken to improve "student learning."

A final note about utilizing educational textbooks: They are an excellent source of "how to." For the most part, the authors have extensive knowledge of the material they are presenting in the text, but many times that can be a detriment instead of a help. For instance, an author who too briefly emphasizes the importance or application and spends the majority of the written material on the concept itself. This is not necessarily bad however many times it is minimally useful in the "interest promotion" process. The problem I see too often is experts in their field write the texts used in courses and they spend most of the text on the mechanics of whatever they are presenting. Introductory paragraphs or explanations rarely explain sufficiently and convincingly why and how this affects the reader and therefore does not do much to generate reader interest. The experts are so focused on the mechanics of the presentation, which rightfully is of great interest to them, the basic motivation is generally thought to be expected rather than needed to be generated. This is where the teacher must compliment the text and not ignore what seems academic to them. The writers of course texts have an extreme interest in the subject because it interests them. Such may not be the case for new learners/readers and must be significantly reinforced by the teacher. This, again, is part of course planning and takes time to develop, which is probably why it is not as common a practice as it should be. Generating student interest is the foremost promotion of learning that a teacher can make. Too many times as an administrator, I have witnessed the converse and, because of legal protective roadblocks built into the system, the converse persists. There are few things more important in the responsibilities of the teacher than instilling a believable need to learn.

A Thought

If we put the responsibility and accountability for student learning on the teacher, we can logically expect to get a greater overall commitment to classroom learning. The converse is also true and is a major part of the problem preventing us from becoming the foremost leader in education in the world. Clear thinking says we cannot solve problems if we don't know what they are because a perceived necessity for any improvement is truly the mother of invention; in government, business, or an educational classroom. If we have to, we will find a way to improve. If we do not have to, especially when due to a lack of accountability and continuous improvement, then complacency breeds. The unfortunate part is the student ultimately carries the consequence of complacency—poor learning. We, as educational teachers, leaders, etc., must be responsible and accountable for what we produce!

Reforms to Teach More Effectively

- ▶ Accept personal and professional responsibility for student learning.
- ▶ Inspire student motivation and generate a cause to learn for all course topics.

- Create measureable objectives for all major course topics.
- Teach by ethically utilizing all three modes of learning receptivity for all course objectives.
- Document a "class grade average," grading the level of learning of all course measureable objectives and resultant teaching effectiveness, for each assigned course.
- Compute the "class grade average," using comprehensive final examination grades or cumulative test grades; all enrolled students—no exemptions.
- Prepare a continuous teaching improvement plan; evaluating individual course measureable objectives versus corresponding class examination/test grades.

CHAPTER 3: TEACH TO ENSURE LEARNING

ENSURING LEARNING

The age-old questions: How do we learn? How do we know something? How do we know we know something? What process do we go through to put something into our mind, then recall it from our mind, and then apply what we recalled? It would appear the whole notion of "learning" would have to include the aforementioned: putting something into our mind, recalling it, and then applying it. One's varying ability to do that would then reflect a level of learning. Now, what is the process we go through? The most accepted research on learning says people put information into our minds by a combination of hearing, seeing, and/or feeling it. Please note: just hearing, seeing, and feeling information does not in itself constitute learning. These are only the "modes" we use to communicate information into our, and/or others, minds. There is general acceptance in teaching practice if we actually apply the information we heard, saw, and/or felt, we would tend to remember it—meaning we could recall and apply it when needed; thus learned it. It would be reasonable to deduce the more times we applied the same information we heard, saw, and/or felt, we would have "learned it" to a greater level.

The first important point in observing teaching is to examine how teachers generally go about communicating information to the student. The norm seems to be to tell it by verbal instruction (expounding, urging—lecture): identified in this text as "preaching." This appears to justify the first mode, hearing. The seeing mode is intended to be justified by visually demonstrating something related to the topic. In education, this is usually implemented by using different media mechanisms such as a white board, computer screen, etc. Unfortunately, these mechanisms really represent the hearing mode—the student is repeating it to themselves, what they are reading from the board or computer, and thus hear himself or herself. The feeling mode, again unfortunately and deficiently, is more often than not left out of most general education teaching—the excuse being "it does not relate well" to general education subjects except for writing as a physical application, and that is really stretching the imagination for receiving information through feeling. That is about as flimsy a representation as the whiteboard is to meeting the information receptive mode of seeing. Now, here we are getting to the nature of the teaching/learning problem in our culture. Remember that hearing, seeing, and feeling are the most accepted modes used to enter information into our minds; however, that alone does not constitute learning! We also know each of us naturally receive and process information at different levels of reception via the three modes. Some of us do well with hearing, versus others who do better with seeing, versus others with feeling, even though we physically have and tend to use one, to all three abilities. However, these receptive modes appear to change in priority given the situation. We tend to receive information in reaction to the way it was sent. A person burning their hand on a stove will receive the burn information immediately through the feeling mode even though they may be hearing mode biased. In addition, a person's frantic motions received through the seeing mode may take precedence over a feeling bias. Overall, we tend to use the three modes to receive and process information although we individually have differing, and in some cases significant personal biases, utilizing those modes. *It only makes sense we would receive and retain information more effectively if all three modes were used to send it. That is an important basis for effective instruction. In other words, we can reach more people/students utilizing all three receptive modes.*

Again, our current educational problem is exacerbated by the deceptive teaching notion of success using the verbal teaching method alone. This is justified by interpretation of test grades that plot a bell shaped curve thereby documenting accepted learning variance within the class. Contrary to this notion is that those students with the stronger receptive modes of seeing and feeling are in trouble right from the start. This major problem has initiated many other problems in our educational system, hence those students biased in the other modes of information reception logically tend to receive lower grades, or become the students perceived as those who "just can't learn." It has been my experience, through interviews, the "just can't learn" students are usually the students who return to school after being in the world of work, finding they can learn by using the other modes of seeing and/or feeling; and because they were successful, why can't they go back to school and do well—in spite of the teachers? Many do, and tend to do it very well. I believe the seeing and/or feeling biased learners have significantly experienced converting on-the-job hearing information into seeing and/or feeling practical applications at work and thus are/were more successful learning (putting information into their mind, recalling, and applying it) than they ever were at school. *They actually wound up doing the job the formal schoolteacher should have done.* Do you see where this is heading?

I once had a young math teacher we hired tell me his goal in teaching math was to take the class to the school lab and teach students math by showing how it is really derived and applied in real life. I remember him saying math should only be taught in the lab (applying all three receptive modes) where it is used. Incidentally, he meant a real-life industrial practical applications lab which his school had, not the traditional math lab with only computers programmed to reinforce the preaching methodology. This person's intent coincided with the accepted educational theory that students "can" receive information more effectively utilizing the three modes; multivariate. Also remember I said "can" receive information, I did not say they would receive it. What do I mean by that?

Today's students appear to respond significantly different from yesterday's students! The technology ease of making available large amounts of information has drastically changed the attention span of most people. If it interests them, they continue to read and or see

Chapter 3: Teach To Ensure Learning

on. If not, they hit "mental delete" and move on to the next item of initial interest. This conditioning directly relates to the learning behavior of the student in the classroom. If they are interested in the topic presented, and they are biased in the mode of presentation, they will probably do better than those disinterested will and/or biased otherwise. The real key here is "if they are interested." If not interested, regardless of their learning mode bias, they will probably tend to tune out the presentation and focus some of their thoughts elsewhere, not able to receive and retain enough information to start the recall and application process—learning. Since the attention span of the student today is so much shorter than that of yesteryear, it is necessary for the successful teacher to develop interest in the topic right from the start—of any concepts and/or topics they are presenting.

Teaching, according to various dictionary definitions, is to "impart knowledge" and/or to "ensure to learn." Unfortunately, that is how we exacerbated our learning problems: by only "imparting knowledge" through preaching, all interest aside, and if students remember it okay and if not tough! Too many teachers feel their job is only to present the information and the rest is up to the individual student. If they recall it for the tests, then we assume they have learned it. Typical advice (unfortunate for those who are biased other than hearing) is to read it, study it, go over it many times in your mind so you remember it for the test. In today's "real world" that does not appear to work well. Attitude, time available, family structure, interest, environment, etc. are all affecting factors. I believe to be an effective teacher one has the responsibility to impart knowledge in the most effective way, ultimately resulting in learning by the student. *Good teaching has to ensure learning.* If we focus on ensuring learning, we can resolve the problems currently plaguing us. So, what do we have to do to ensure student learning?

First: Develop an interest in the required topic. Find a way to show the learner how it will affect them in an important way. One sentence as to the relevance of the topic "doesn't work!" Most people's attention is gained when the nature of the topic affects something important to them. Incidentally, threatening to give students an "F" grade does not promote interest and may actually promote the reverse. Topics necessary to be presented in classrooms or elsewhere generally have a beginning point. Someone discovered that knowledge somewhere and for some purpose. Example: Where and/or why did the subject of Algebra develop? Where and/or why the Pythagorean Theorem? Where and/or why does a minus times a minus equal a plus, etc.? These beginning points, "where and/or why," are usually of interest to learners, **especially when related to "how" they seriously affect us today.** Another problem is most teachers don't even know where/why/how those things were invented or developed. *It behooves the teacher to know and present real interest in the topic in order to develop a reasoning to learn.* People, even students, have to have a reason to want to do something. Learning something one sees no purpose in is a lost endeavor, defeated before starting, and much of today's preach-teaching without convincing purpose, is very successful at that!

Second: Teach all topics utilizing all three receptive modes: hearing, seeing, and feeling. A lot of forethought, known as "teacher preparation," will have to go into the design and implementation of this. The importance of this rule cannot be over stressed. Even if interested, if the student does not receive information on their "wavelength" some will be lost and experience greater difficultly in learning. The person who told me their elementary grade teacher was having trouble with the students understanding the process of averaging numbers gave an example of the power of all three modes. In desperation, he marched the whole class to the school gym where they had the final scores of all their school's basketball games posted on the wall. The subsequent teaching and learning is obvious but the important point here was twofold. The teacher engaged the students in all three modes of learning and the result was an adult who never forgot the experience, and/or the learning that took place because of it. Another glaring example was a freshman college class in Educational Psychology 101 where the teacher gave each student the option of attending the lecture class twice a week, or going to the local halfway house for four hours per week and report writing per course instructions. Who do you think learned more about educational psychology in that class? The students at the halfway house who certainly were exposed to all three modes of learning, or those listening to the preached-hearing mode only? See the value of the three modes of perception? Not presenting information utilizing those modes is almost derelict to the profession of teaching and certainly detrimental to the learning of the student.

Third: Test for recall and application of each measurable objective, then evaluate and re-teach were necessary, utilizing all three modes again. The given test after the teaching process is completed is not to grade the student, but to show the teacher what deficiencies exist in the teaching information flow, learning recall, and application process. This gives the teacher the necessary opportunity to improve by going back and re-teaching those items for better student learning. It serves as a teacher self-check and is necessary for the teacher's continuous instructional improvement.

Fourth: Retest again for grading. The overall class results of the grading, personal name identification withheld, should be publicly available information. It is important for a teacher to develop the mental philosophy that the only failure in the classroom will be the teacher! *It is the teacher's job to ensure learning of the students.* Effective teachers do take their responsibility personally. If students are failing in the class, then the teacher is failing. Look at all the great teachers in history. They all seem to follow the pattern of effective teaching previously outlined. They always developed interest in their various teachings which set the stage for learning. Their teachings were filled with seeing and feeling experiences, so much so that books thousands of years later still describe them. They even tested the applications of their student's learning in numerous ways.

Throughout my career, I have met a number of extremely effective teachers and they all had similar things in common. Their first concern was always student learning. Even the students knew—they felt it! They were hands-on, they always developed instruction using the three modes, and their test results reflected their efforts. Few failures, if any, and always the highest perceived evaluation. The subjects included math and chemistry, traditionally known for high levels of difficulty. An example of one teacher's commitment to ensure learning was a high school chemistry classroom with the ceiling totally covered with chemical nomenclature-lattice diagrams. When asked what the ceiling diagrams were for the teacher said he told all the students if they ever fell asleep in his class the chemical designations would be the first thing they would see when their heads went upright and their eyes opened; a must in their learning! From that, those students felt and knew his commitment to their learning and developed a greater interest in the teacher and the subject. Incidentally, students know who the good teachers are, and do we really have to ask ourselves why that is?

In conclusion: In order to reform teaching and learning in America, we must teach to ensure learning, and prove it! Anything less is cheating the students' opportunity to learn. *"The only failure in the classroom is the teacher."*

A THOUGHT

"How to get students to learn?" The applied psychology I have read, heard, seen, and actually experienced indicates a practical answer to those questions, in the real world, is to *change ourselves*. The reaction to *our change* tends to elicit a change in others. What we do, and how we do it motivates others—for the good or for the bad! I do not believe there is a status quo in this we are either going positive or negative all the time. We change to elicit a corresponding change in others and when our change disappears, we are back to the original situation.

I have experienced students are much more, or significantly more, perceptive than most teachers ever give them credit for. They know and respond to the attitude, personality, and persona the teacher displays, *consciously and/or unconsciously*. Why is it that a seemingly small frail elderly teacher can hold a class of 35 plus energetic high school combined gender students spellbound and attentive versus the opposite person's physical stature, with opposite subsequent results? The students' perception of the teacher and their resultant behavior must be in reaction to whatever the teacher displays, does, or has done. I believe the students' perception of non-verbal teacher characteristics is much more related to their classroom behavior (learning included) than we can imagine. If students perceive and believe you are concerned about their individual learning, then their attitude towards accepting or learning what you are teaching appears to be more instinctively motivated, or more positively influenced, which leads one to believe their level of learning will be greater. On the other hand, if a teacher is extremely effective in delivering the information being taught, but the students' perception of the teacher is threatening or impersonal, then the level of learning is decreased from what it could and/or should be.

The influence of the teacher's "personal commitment to their individual learning," *as perceived and believed by students*, is probably the most learning related motivational factor in the classroom. This is overlooked and yet a significant factor relating to student learning. It is something very difficult to be taught for a teacher to do. It appears to me it is intrinsic to the character, personality, persona, and commitment of the person teaching. Excellent teachers have it and others do not. Maybe that is why the excellent teachers most often do their job in spite of the pay, than because of it. They love their job responsibility, student learning, and the students know, believe, and are motivated to learn because of it. I have witnessed this characteristic of excellent teachers so many times in my career and believe it would be difficult to be packaged, bagged, and sold by any teacher education programs. Excellent teachers have it; others have to work harder to try to display/achieve it. Students, as well as others, react to what they see, feel, and hear! *Sound familiar?*

Now, the more we can do, the "reforms" we have to make, to assure these types of teachers are the greater majority employed, is the subject of this book. It is not so much how we identify these excellent teachers but the "reforms" we have to implement to identify the poorer teachers, then continuously improve them or replace them with more effective teachers, to significantly increase "student learning."

REFORMS TO ENSURE LEARNING

- Ethically incorporate all three receptive learning modes for teaching all course measurable objectives.

- Create genuine student interest in all course objectives and abolish threats of failure or threats of any kind.

- Create intermittent course tests to measure student learning and evaluate teaching effectiveness of all major course objectives. Utilize the results for the improvement of instruction, such as re-teaching, versus student grading.

- Display a recognizable classroom attitude and demeanor that the teacher's primary priority is "student learning."

Chapter 4: Teacher Evaluation

The Process

The questions should be: "How are teachers currently evaluated?" and "How should teachers be evaluated?"

How are teachers currently evaluated? The prevailing processes I have witnessed over 22 years in education are far removed from evaluating teaching performance based on student learning. First, most learning institutions and school districts have their own faculty evaluation systems "conjured up" by drafting and redrafting until approval is reached among faculty organizations, unions, administration, etc. You can believe they are non-threatening in order to gain the approval of all constituent groups, therefore, a variety of categories make up the evaluation.

The contents of an evaluation can typically include: *First,* a peer evaluation whereby a peer faculty member observes classroom presentations and writes a report; *Second,* an administrative observation of classroom performance where an administrator observes classroom performance and reports—usually once/twice a semester, announced and/or unannounced according to the faculty agreement for that institution/district; *Third,* a student evaluation of faculty which typically reflects the student's perception of the faculty member; and *Fourth,* a faculty member's self-report of activities, etc. All the evaluation items are generally put together and then reviewed between the faculty member and their supervisor and/or a committee made up of reviewers. I believe the current process is certainly comprehensive; utilizing all parties concerned, but the real and most important focus of what the evaluation should be is totally missed, overlooked, and/or ignored. *A faculty evaluation, specifically relating to the teacher's foremost job responsibility, must reveal the level of classroom student learning achieved; all documented by testing based on comprehensive measurable objectives of the course.*

I do not recall ever seeing overall classroom student learning documented per specific objectives and then analyzed as part of a faculty member's performance evaluation, let alone being used as a basis for improvement. The logical outcome of teaching is *student learning* and that is what the faculty member is paid for. Now, how was the logical and most important faculty responsibility missed? I believe this primary responsibility has been increasingly camouflaged over time by layered bureaucratic school systems verbally shifting the responsibility for classroom outcomes to the consumer (the student). They are successful at doing it because most parents, consumers, or whoever feel inadequate to disagree. *The public's ingrained perception of a teacher appears to be not to question them or the principal, and to stay out of the principal's office!* Who, as a consumer, has the nerve to ask the teacher to show their effectiveness ranking documented by student class grades? Students resist asking because they perceive the teacher may retaliate against them. Parents resist because they perceive the teacher may retaliate against their children. Asking the principal or department head usually winds up in the standard answer, "We already have a comprehensive evaluation system blah, blah, blah." *Someone, sometime has to stand up to the teachers, administrators, and school board and persistently demand to be shown the level of student learning and resultant level of teacher effectiveness taking place in all classes. It can be documented specifically by computing a class grade average based on a comprehensive final examination or cumulative test grades; representing the student level of achievement of the course measureable objectives.* As a paying consumer, it seems logical one should be able to see what is received for the money. I believe the school would be dumbfounded; they would not know where to begin; no records of tests/exams tied to specific and comprehensive course objectives, teacher performance related to student learning non-existent, thus teacher effectiveness rating not available. Again, I realize somewhere and sometime someone in our nation's school districts is actually reviewing student learning and tying it to faculty evaluation and that is a great step forward, but that process, from what I have witnessed, is few and far between and almost nonexistent—I applaud anyone doing it.

    I have actually attended a required faculty review session where all the parties gave their input and a reviewer in the group, who was appointed by a new rule asking for input from outside the normal faculty members group, stood up and said (I will try to paraphrase), "This is a total joke. This faculty member is not doing the job and should be replaced, but you people are afraid to do anything because you have to work with him/her and you are scared of the unions/legal/personal repercussions." He was upset and stalked out of the review disgusted. Needless to say, the faculty member being reviewed had real problems and should have been replaced, but because of the review process (which subsequently supported and applauded his/her performance) he/her continued to repeat as "the only failure in the classroom." Imagine the student learning that was neglected, year after year, because of a system that never even entertained the idea of reviewing what and how the students learned from this teacher. How can we as a nation be a leader in education when we do not evaluate and make subsequent improvement decisions based on how well the students learn from their teacher? Our current system is not missing the boat; we act as though we do not even know where the boat is. It is only logical to base the effectiveness of a teacher on how well their students learn. We appear to be doing everything but!

How should teachers be evaluated? It is more than obvious the lack of teachers being evaluated based on the learning of their students is a major part of the education dilemma in the United States. That is how we promote poor teaching and subsequent poorer learning. How many jobs/professions are there where the persons paid to perform a task are not evaluated on the outcome of that task? Darn few! Even politicians are reviewed on the effects of their performance, at the voting booth. If they perform poorly, they are gone. Look at the professions of sales, entertainment, construction, transportation, etc. Persons performing tasks are evaluated on the outcome of those tasks. That is how whatever is produced is improved! Note, the end of the Second World War brought about a manufacturing revolution in Japan. After the war, the products produced in Japan were commonly referred to as junk! People purposely looked for the signature quotation, "Made in USA," before they purchased, otherwise they were taking a chance on buying a product that would fall apart or fail. Then, thanks to an American statistician, Dr. Edwards Deming, Japanese manufacturing adopted an improvement process. In general, they documented what they produced, then evaluated that documentation, and thus made subsequent improvements. They repeated this process "continuously" and thus improved the products they made. Their reformation from producing junk to producing some of the best products in the world is common knowledge and is an example of what can be accomplished through objective evaluation of productivity. Am I comparing apples to oranges: manufacturing to teaching? You miss the point if you think that! I am reinforcing the logical concept that to improve what you produce, you must document what you produce, evaluate it, and then improve it. Now, what do teachers produce? The result of the teaching process is the learning by the student. That is the product of what teachers produce: student learning! Teacher organizations, government studies, accreditation agencies, etc. can and do produce continual rhetoric that fogs and/or expands the basic responsibility of the teacher. So much so the initial and foremost responsibility of the teacher, "student learning," is ignored. In reality, no matter what protective groups conjure up about a teacher's responsibility, the bottom line to the consumer and/or parent is, "What learning took place?" Are we paying the teacher for preaching or for student learning? The answer has to be "student learning." It only makes sense; we pay the teacher to teach a class, the teacher teaches and nobody knows what overall level of learning took place in the class. Yes, grades are given to individual students, but where are all the final examination grades, reflecting the achievement of the course objectives, published? They document the teaching effectiveness and resultant level of learning that took place in the class. Yes, I said, "Published!" Alternatively, the teacher usually receives a print out of all the final course grades given (*not the final exam grades*) however I do not recall ever even seeing that print out, notoriously erroneous to verifiable student learning, used as a primary and/or credible basis for teacher evaluation.

Now, I am sure somewhere, sometime, evaluation based on verifiable student learning might take place, but it does not appear common place and is strongly resisted by teacher representative organizations. Do you wonder why? First, to document what the students have learned, and the effectiveness of the teacher, we have to test the student's knowledge and/or performance of course objectives. How can we improve any process, teaching included, unless we document what we are producing and use that as a basis for determining and/or improving our performance. Again, the problem is that teachers are not evaluated on the learning of their students. In fact, most evaluation systems of faculty are far removed from any documented learning that took place in their class. The closest I have seen is a "Student Evaluation of Faculty Survey" that focuses on the student's perception of their teacher. This is far removed from documenting the level of learning that took place in the class. The learning that takes place in the class has to be the prime focus of the teacher and the level of learning should serve as the documented basis of teacher performance. This information must then be used in teaching improvement planning and faculty appointment decision making. If we want to be a world leader in education, we have to have the best teachers. That is, teachers who are able to promote the highest level of student learning given the objectives of their course and documented by formal and comprehensive testing.

Education has to focus on "student learning." If we focus on "student learning," then the teaching that takes place in and to different groups (socioeconomic, urban, rural, etc.) will have to be varied and different to elicit the highest level of learning from those individual and varied groups of learners. Different methods for different groups! The converse is obvious: If we continue to preach-teach, similar to all groups, then we will reap what we have sown; higher level of learning from those students/groups who adapt to preach-teach and total failure from those that do not. The effect of this is a matter of record and must be changed. One shoe size does not fit all and that must be the challenge of the teacher, to elicit the highest level of learning from different groups, and different teaching methods for different groups.

My good and late friend, who I shall call Dr. Ed, told me his biggest challenge was teaching math to a group of immigrants whose country of origin lacked formal education. He said he gave up on the formal classroom format for this group and took them outside on the rear school lawn and, using the required math course concepts, related those concepts to crop planting processes (something they could relate to because of their agricultural background) to teach the objectives of the course. Yes, they grew crops, learned math, and met the objectives of the course. Dr. Ed was elated the level of learning was so high in a group that no other teacher wanted to even begin to teach. Now, imagine the planning Dr. Ed had to do to relate the learning environment to the objectives of the course and the difficult background of the students. Dr. Ed truly believed the only failure in the classroom was the teacher and he is genuinely missed. Thanks, Dr. Ed!

To improve student learning I would expect teacher administrators to require documentation and evaluation of how course topic objectives relate to corresponding class examination/test grades, in each teacher's course. The graphical representation of those grades versus objectives would present immediate recognition of teaching methods, if any, that need to be improved. That should be the major part of the teacher's continuous improvement plan. Also, the faculty member's class grade average based on a comprehensive final examination or cumulative tests, for all enrolled students, should be made public. This would document the student level of learning and the teacher's effectiveness. The public is paying for learning and currently cannot even find out how much, or how well, learning took place. No, I do not buy the argument we should only know our own, or our own children scores. The teacher's paid responsibility is for student learning and the teacher teaches a class, so what student learning took place in the class? We have to know in order to evaluate and improve. Face it; it also serves as a motivation tool for teachers to focus on student learning instead of preach-teaching. It is time to reverse the roles and put the consumer in charge of evaluating what they purchase. Public employees work for the public, not some intermediate organization that shields them from public scrutiny. The bottom line is we have to change our system's philosophical focus from preach-teach to documented "student learning," and then we will be on the road to "Reforming Education for the Real World.

A THOUGHT

A parent is concerned because their child received a low grade in a course at school and approaches the teacher for an explanation. After due discourse the parent walks away convinced the low grade is well deserved and probably feels guilty they are part of the cause.

On the other hand, the parent could/should ask to see the corresponding grades of all the other students (names omitted) and how those grades compare to their child's grades relative to each specific course objective measured. This would document deficient areas and justify discussion regarding future improvement. Also, is this the only student in the class who received a low grade? If so, then there might be merit to the teacher's reasoning however if not, then there might be other causes. What is the teacher's effectiveness rating as well as the school's minimum acceptable level of student learning for a class (a class graded average based on a comprehensive final exam or cumulative test grades), and how does it relate to this class? If the teacher refuses to show the class examination grades (names omitted) then it would never be known if this low level of performance is isolated or a trend. This, in turn, does not lend itself to continuous improvement and only further alienates the consumer. Most excellent teachers I know have no problem documenting their effectiveness and generally will when discussing grade problems with parents or students. The converse usually holds true and therein lies the problem! As an educational consumer, it is best to check the depth of the water before diving into the pool. If prior student learning documentation and resultant teacher effectiveness ratings do not exist, then education decision making to the consumer is just a gamble. This will have to change in order to significantly and continuously improve teaching and learning, as well as meet consumer demands for the "real world!"

REFORM TEACHER EVALUATION

- Document measurable course objectives for all major course topics taught.
- Document comprehensive final examinations and cumulative tests that include all major course measurable objectives, for all courses taught.
- Document a "class grade average" for each assigned course, grading the class level of learning and resultant teaching effectiveness.
- Compute the "class grade average" using the comprehensive final examination grades or cumulative test grades: all enrolled students, no exemptions.
- Prepare a continuous teaching improvement plan; evaluating individual course measureable objectives versus corresponding class examination/test grades.
- Demonstrate re-appointment based on acceptable class grade averages in the most recent classes, and an acceptable continuous teaching improvement plan.

Chapter 5: Teacher Contracts

Types and Content

This chapter will focus directly on the effects of teacher contracts, what they currently are, and what they should be. I say "should be" because they should relate to student learning and currently they do not. Note the legal contents of teacher contracts may and will vary from state to state, but the outcome of awarding a contract, and how that directly affects student learning, is what is most important. Remember, the public educational institution is, or should be, in business for one overall reason only: *student learning!*

Typically, there are two main types of full-time faculty teaching contracts used in public education:

First: Probationary Contract. This is written for faculty who have not completed a probationary period, but are employed in a tenure granting position; better described as a "tenure track" appointment. Generally, probation periods for tenure track faculty vary from two to seven years, depending on the particular school, school district, college, and/or university.

Probationary faculty should be, and are, subject to administrative review of their performance prior to awarding every new annual probationary contract. The school administration generally has the right to not renew a probationary contract without showing cause. In other words, they do not have to give a reason for not renewing a contract and can terminate the faculty employment whenever and for whatever they choose. However, this is not always the case in a probationary appointment, as a faculty member in say the 5th or 6th year of a 7-year tenure granting position has gained legal support in some states for requiring the institution to show cause, even though they are not bound to. The reasoning for this is if the institution has employed them for four years or so without documented problems, meaning their performance was acceptable, they should be given a chance to correct any deficiencies cited before the tenure decision. Therefore, the early years in the probationary appointment are now being focused on more intently because once the faculty member has completed the probationary process, and is tenured (tenure decisions vary among institutions from somewhat automatic to exceedingly selective) it is the school's responsibility to show cause for non-contract renewal. This process, as discussed further in this chapter, can be, and generally is, a huge and significant impediment to student learning.

Second: Tenured Faculty Continuing Contract. This appears to be an automatic contract renewal awarded annually, only subject to a show cause process that appears to be avoided by schools in lieu of struggling with the problem, rather than dealing with it.

More often than not, the legal process of a non-acceptable tenured faculty performance issue is so cumbersome and time delaying that most schools avoid it at all costs. In effect, the only way I have seen a tenured faculty member terminated is by the faculty member committing a felony, then they are placed on administrative leave pending the outcome of the judicial process. If convicted of the felony, they are terminated. If not convicted, then the tenured faculty member generally resumes their school duties. Any non-acceptable performance, other than the commission of a felony, is disputable and winds up in lengthy review between the tenured faculty member and the school administration. Again, more often than not, this process takes years to work through given that the school must provide remedial education and/or training for the tenured faculty member based on the notion the faculty member's performance during the probation period was acceptable, and because it is not acceptable now, must be the responsibility of the school. The poor performance in question is determined to be the school's responsibility, therefore the school must provide remedial education and/or training to bring the poor performance back from poor to acceptable.

An employer's acceptance of this "legally generated" performance solution is certainly debatable! Here is the despicable problem! All the time the remedial education and/or retraining continues the student classes continue, semester after semester, with the poor faculty performance continuing without anyway of stopping it. Even if the courses taught by the faculty member could be staffed by someone else, which is generally not the case because there are just not enough faculty to cover extra contingencies/areas of expertise like this, the faculty member in question could and most likely would file a formal grievance against his/her replacement and is returned to the classroom to inflict more damage pending the outcome of the grievance and the retraining. Exceptions to this include assigning the faculty member in question non-questionable duties for the review/repair period at a double cost to the school (replacement plus faculty member salary in question).

The damage inflicted by unacceptable performance of tenured teachers (documented by poor level of student learning) is immeasurable! This includes not only poor classroom teaching and/or student learning but also *resistance to course and program revisions, incorporating new technology, and other curriculum changes advised by external advisory groups and/or school administration.* Resistance to such changes, and in many cases just outright refusal, results in promoting student learning obsolescence along with the start of a lengthy legal show cause complaint against the faculty member. This legal process usually winds up causing polarization of faculty supporters/non-supporters which increases internally due to the lengthy duration of legal wrangling, and many times the end result appears to be worse than the initial problem itself, even though it is not because the ultimate loser is the student. That is one of the major reasons school administrations, more often than not, do not pursue specific and necessary changes. Again, legal avoidance of tenured faculty poor performance only promotes and eventually leads to obsolescence, the direct opposite of the concept of continuous improvement. I have witnessed teacher tenure is nothing more than a legal contractual situation that prevents school administration from acting, let alone acting quickly, to resolve poor teacher performance and, in the cases of poor teacher performance, is a major impediment to student learning.

Here are some of the current arguments in favor of the tenure process:

- *Protection from being fired for personal, political, or other reasons.*
- *Stops schools from replacing high cost teachers with low cost new teachers.*
- *Protects teachers for teaching controversial topics.*
- *Promises a secure profession.*
- *Tenure is a reward for positive prior teaching evaluations.*
- *Protects faculty by lay-off related to and by seniority.*

This list goes on and on with all kinds of reasons teachers should be a protected group. **Take particular note there is no relationship to documented student learning in the tenure arguments and that in itself is, and if not should be, the primary job responsibility of the Teacher.** How many of you readers out there in the real world have employment, a job, or profession that strongly and legally protects you from being fired or replaced except for the commission of a felony? Even a self-employed person has to answer to their customers! It does not make sense to promote poor teaching by guaranteeing continuing employment of underperforming teachers. Teacher representative groups will say this is not true, there is a process for resolving poor teaching problems. Sure, *the process may take years* if it is successful, is riddled with legal ping-pong wrangling, is a major institutional morale distraction with monumental documentation and reviews, and generally winds up with the students, semester after semester until resolved, suffering the most; a process ill-conceived to resolve teacher problems, actually creates more problems, and then amplifies them. Tenure only benefits the teachers and has little educational value for the students, and is significantly detrimental to student learning. ***Teacher contracts must be based on performance of the teacher's job responsibility: producing an acceptable level of documented student learning.***

If the students are not learning at an acceptable level, based on approved measurable course objectives and resulting testing, then require teaching improvement planning and implementation or replace the teacher. Not doing this is almost criminal in nature, knowing poor teaching resulting in negative student learning is taking place. Remember, students move on, semester to semester, and build on the prior learning accomplished. If learning in a particular semester was significantly poor, they are at an extreme disadvantage in the forthcoming class. Unfortunately, awareness and action to halt this type of detrimental damage is typically overlooked when evaluating faculty and renewing contracts, significantly so when the teacher is protected by tenure. Documented student learning, when below an acceptable level, and the subsequent negative effects, are rarely factors conditional in tenured faculty reappointment. *Is the teacher's job conditional on the learning of the students? No! Should it be? Yes!* If you are paying the costs of education, which you are (taxes and/or tuition or both), it certainly makes sense it should be. Try not performing, or performing poorly at your job, and see what happens! Proponents of tenure argue teachers are well

Chapter 5: Teacher Contracts

evaluated by students, other faculty, and administration, and all of these are taken into account in the appointment process. Be aware this type of evaluation process is the problem! Not the solution! First off, "Student Evaluation of Faculty" (SEF's) do not document student learning. They are only the student's perception of the faculty member *before the final grade is given!* The relationship between a favorable student perception of the teacher and documented testing/learning of approved course objectives may, and possibly can be, quite different. Many times I have heard tenured faculty lament they had great students in the class (in reverse the students had a great perception of the teacher) but the students were just too slow to learn and specific course material was left out. There was no documented course objectives testing to uncover the lack of teaching/learning, the teacher received high evaluation scores, and the students moved on lacking what they should have known. As a result, the tenured faculty member moves on to engage a new class with similar performance, and a new contract year with the same old problem. Class after class and somewhere down the line the student faces the fact they have a problem and must accelerate their learning to catch up what they have missed, or just say it is now too difficult and drop out. All of this down the line is directly related back to poor learning in a prior class and what is worse, it is allowed to continue because of legally guaranteed jobs: "tenure." In reality and practice, the tenure process guarantees, in the case of some and/or many faculty, the perpetuation of poor teacher performance resulting in poor student learning and is one of the major root causes of a failing educational system. Remember, many states do have a show cause requirement for non-reappointment of tenured faculty however, traditional "union bargaining contracts" just make the "show cause" process more difficult because the job responsibility of attaining an acceptable level of documented student learning is not a requirement for reappointment. I contend, in general, the more difficult it is to hold teachers accountable for documented student learning the poorer the education outcomes for students will be in that system/district/unit.

So What Do We Have To Do? *Directly relate teacher reappointment contracts to documented student learning.* That way the school would only be reappointing proven teachers, in that their students learn and document their learning through administrative approved course objectives and resultant testing. Now, I can hear the cries of opponents arguing the teacher's job is just not teaching! To me that not only implies, but also is in actuality, the reason student learning is seriously subjugated or overlooked as the paramount teaching job responsibility and is the nature of the overall problem, not the solution. Teachers contend because their job may include meetings, paid retraining, coaching, counseling, study groups, professional organizations, etc., that faculty must have a spread out evaluation focusing on all their duties. This usually winds up in a pro-rated evaluation process that obliterates and/or demotes "student learning" to a non-accountable, *and in most cases non-existent,* weight of performance. The current teacher evaluation process is generally called "comprehensive" and is a designated pro-rated review process including peer review, administrative review, student evaluation of faculty (SEF's) professional involvements, etc. However, *the whole concept of documenting what and how well the student has learned is lost in the forest for* *the trees.* To make matters worse, the actual documentation of what and how well the students learned, in the classes the faculty member is responsible for, is either not available, ignored, or subjugated to a laundry list of the other so called priority items, agreed upon by a bargaining unit or a committee. What deception! ***In all the years I spent as a faculty member or administrator I never remember being involved in a faculty evaluation that compared collective student class grades to comprehensive course objectives for the purpose of instructional improvement.*** How such a basic job responsibility is overlooked is a tribute to years of padding the faculty evaluation bill to focus on everything but student learning.

Unfortunately, the current faculty evaluation process leads to school praise of some faculty members who have no business in a classroom, and only reinforces their poor performance. It actually makes it harder to remove them because of this type of erroneous evaluation documentation. I have seen a case where documentation of poor teaching had been so well documented the district/school board refused to take action for removal because the administrative documentation would appear "biased." Again, another faculty member teaching in a position where they have no business being. Bad enough they are in a position they should not be in, but think of the damage they are inflicting to the learners.

Make "teacher contracts" subject to documented student learning! Even at that rate the satisfactory amount or level of student learning will be debated and verbalized by so many in the venue that, in itself, will constitute a major debate. At least the appointment of teachers to classes will be based on what and how the student's learn from that teacher. This is the way it should be in the *real world* and not concealed by a laundry list of other so-called responsibilities. There is no greater teacher responsibility than of what and how well the students learned in the class. That is the bottom line and should be the only significant basis for appointment and/or no appointment. Anything less just degrades accountability and degrades the teaching effectiveness of the school, and the education system it represents. Our present system is an excellent example of what happens when poor learning, predicated on poor teaching, is allowed to take place. Think of the improvement it would make if teachers were appointed on how well their students learned the documented material they are responsible for. Student's final examination grades or cumulative tests, reflecting the level of learning of all course objectives and resultant teaching effectiveness, would tell the whole story. Anything else is just a cover-up, and an injustice to the customer/consumer: the student!

A Thought

Fortunately, I like to believe the major amount of faculty at an institution of learning are professional teachers dedicated to their profession and make reasonable efforts to work with administration to resolve problems and stay current in their individual fields of study. The problems that do occur generally occur with a minority of the faculty, which unfortunately take up to 90 percent of inconsequential managerial and legal time. During this time consuming process, the collateral damage inflicted within the school too many times becomes intolerable. People become alienated, faculty and staff take sides, others become involved in issues

Chapter 5: Teacher Contracts

because of friendships and involve parents and/or board members, etc. Therefore, the efforts to improve student learning by replacing a faculty member who's performance is persistently poor but is tenured is most generally avoided. To fix this problem we need to eliminate continuing teacher contracts that are awarded because of the teacher attaining tenure and that have minimal evaluative connection to the job responsibility of student learning. They should be replaced with contracts specifically subject to faculty demonstrating an acceptable level of teacher effectiveness documented by computing a class grade average based on a comprehensive final examination or cumulative tests for each assigned course; all students, no exemptions. This type of contractual employment is much more in keeping with the *real world* accountability of measured performance for success.

REFORM TEACHER CONTRACTS

- Identify all courses the teacher is assigned to teach.
- Require preparation of measurable objectives for all major topics in each course assigned.
- Require comprehensive final course examinations that include all major course measurable objectives, for all students enrolled in all courses assigned, no exemptions.
- Document a "class grade average," grading the level of learning of all course measureable objectives and resultant teaching effectiveness, for each assigned course.
- Compute the "class grade average," using comprehensive final examination grades or cumulative test grades; all enrolled students, no exemptions.

- Demonstrate an acceptable level of teaching effectiveness based on the most recent "class grade averages."
- Prepare a continuous improvement teaching plan; evaluating individual course measureable objectives versus corresponding class examination/test grades.
- Receive, for contract reappointment, approval of all aforementioned requirements.

Chapter 6: Teacher Education

Programs and Learning

How our teachers teach and how students learn is ultimately a product of the teacher education system/process in the United States. For the most part, teachers in the elementary and secondary (High School) systems are required to have a bachelor's degree and a teaching certificate, usually issued by the teacher's individual state. The teaching certification process generally requires the completion of a specific number and type of teacher education, general education, and major area of study courses. Whereas, faculty/professors at the community college, 4-year college, and university systems have individual higher degree requirements but, for the most part, do not require teacher education courses, including "how to teach."

Traditionally the teachers/professors at the community college level have masters degrees and significant job experience in the subjects they are teaching versus the professors at the college/university levels who *generally* have doctorate degrees in their fields of expertise with less real world experience. For elementary and secondary school teachers, the college programs offered in teacher education are somewhat similar in nature but vary in structure. Some states require a student to complete a four-year bachelor's degree in their area of expertise first, and then complete a fifth year teacher education certification program. Other states offer a 4-year teacher education Bachelors Degree program combined with a specific area of expertise. I am sure there are many other variations of education degree programs; the important point is not so much the variation of the programs, but what is taught and learned about teaching in the program. What is taught and learned in the program directly relates to "student learning" and this is the generating nature of the problem we face.

What Do Teacher Education Programs Traditionally Focus On?

Aside from all the psychology and behavioral related coursework, the programs tend to focus on teacher presentation of material, unfortunately through the traditional methodology of lecture (preaching). Education students do study many different teaching methodologies but again, in practice, seem to focus on the old preach-teach. In fact, too many of the traditional teacher education courses are taught using this method. The programs do teach differing methodologies but tend to focus on the traditional verbally failing method of preach-teach. Education students, like the rest of us, tend to learn what they live. If they live by "telling" then they tend to repeat that process. Ironically, science and occupational teachers have been utilizing multi-receptive mode learning for years whereas the traditional "liberal arts" teachers have not. Too many of those teachers unjustly refuse to do the course preparation and implementation work, incorporating all the receptive learning modes of students, because they lack real world experience of how to apply what they are teaching by preaching. How can a teacher teach the application of their material when they have little knowledge of how it is really applied? This is why so many young teachers adopt the textbook method thereby teaching the experience of the author in a verbal format. This is great for verbal learning students with long attention spans but is disaster for others. Additionally, it becomes habit forming and the teacher builds their whole course around the experience of an author and the verbal learning (preaching/reading) experience. Education programs promote and rely so strongly on the textbook learning method they completely overlook the changing learning needs of the students. That is, the same method will not work for all environments including inner city, urban, and rural. In fact, the traditional verbal teaching method is a strong source of the failures, not the answer to the learning problems. In addition, many of the faculty teaching the education programs are products of the preach-teach environment and, in essence, are repeatedly teaching what and how they learned, by example. Yes, many will say if was good enough for them then so be it. Well tell that to the millions of dropouts and stay-outs suffering the wrath of traditional "preach" teaching.

Ever wonder why the proprietary schools are doing so well

today? Look at the way they teach math, science, language, etc. Realistically applied, taught by faculty who are experienced in the use of those subjects every day, in the real world. And yes, they have the same regional accreditation as the public schools and colleges. The traditional thinking is so biased I have actually had a state education official tell me they will never allow that type of proprietary applied learning in their state at the "higher" degree level. If they could, I believe they would stop all proprietary learning as well. I found this to be a revelation, and why the teacher education programs get set on a traditional format and stay there, regardless of need. I believe technology changes rapidly, including student interest, attention spans, environment, etc., but human nature seems to change little and is highly resistant to change. This is the enemy of adaptable teacher education programs and is a major part of the "student learning" problem, not the solution.

What Teacher Education Programs Should Focus On

Simply, teaching teachers how to teach so all students learn! When do we know students have learned? We know students have learned when:

- They remember it.
- They remember how to do it.
- They do it.
- They repeat it.

Note: the level at which they accomplish these steps will identify their level of learning (example: excellent to poor).

Now again, overall and most important, the teacher's

responsibility is "student learning" so they are responsible for *all* their students to:

- Remember it.
- Remember how to do it.
- Do it.
- Repeat it.

So, what should teacher education programs focus on? Initially, teacher education programs must teach prospective teachers how to create and document measurable objectives (what is to be accomplished) for all major topics within a course of study. Subsequent to that, and equally important, how to create and implement multi-receptive learning mode experiences (hearing, seeing, feeling) for those measurable objectives. Multi-receptive learning mode teaching, *for all classes, subjects, and disciplines*, logically increases student learning for *all* students, effecting *all* students to:

- Remember it.
- Remember how to do it.
- Do it.
- Repeat it.

Herein lies the most important operational task of the teacher: to do it! This is what teacher education programs must focus on. Teaching must be based on measurable objectives presented in an *ethical* multi-receptive learning mode format. This should all be created and implemented relative to the type and situation of the students, the background and ingenuity of the teacher, the environment, and many other related factors. It is here good teachers are separated from bad. Those who can create multi-learning mode experiences accomplishing the four previously noted student outcomes are destined to excel in their profession. Those who cannot actually deter student learning and inflict lifelong damage to many. This ability should be decisive at the teacher preparation program level, not years after in an educational institution critical faculty evaluation and subsequent legal due process procedure.

Textbook note: Additionally, and most importantly, textbook learning must be reinforced by the teacher's ingenuity to create multivariate learning mode implementation of the textbook author's intentions. *Textbooks are an excellent guide, but the real responsibility for student learning lies with the teacher's interpretation and created learning experiences to accomplish the textbook concepts.*

INTERPRETING STUDENT TEST RESULTS

Tests! To the student, tests means "my grade." To the parents of students it means, "How well they are learning." To the teacher, too often, it means an entry in their grade books and designates who the "good students" are and who the "poor students" are. *In reality, the tests really show the level at which the students learned the material the teacher was teaching, but more so is documentation of the teacher's effectiveness to ensure student learning.* The teacher must learn from the tests how effective their teaching was and then re-teach, making the necessary changes to ensure learning.

Think of this: If student test scores are plotted on a graph, grades versus number of students with those grades, the traditionally normal accepted distribution creates a bell shaped curve graph.

This generally indicates the class has a small number of extreme scores at a high level "A" and a corresponding small number of low scores "F", or so on. The rest cluster in the middle from B's to D's. Therefore, this is, in too many cases, the *accepted* methodology of grading and even *accepted* to unjustly justify the teacher's proficiency. In too many cases, it is even applied to the overall class test results regardless of overall percentage. What do I mean? The test may consist of 100 questions and instead of grading based on percentage's (100 percent to 75 percent being acceptable grading, below 75 percent failing) the teachers use the highest number of correct answers in the 100 questions as a starting point instead of 100 percent. Say the students take the test and the best score out of the 100 questions is 60, then that is used as an "A" grade and quite possibly the corresponding "F" might reflect only 30 to 40 right answers out of the 100, dependent on the other scores. Logically that means the real student learning of the 100 questions tested is extremely low, but because of the grading method used, is acceptable and justified. Some cases I have seen border on the ridiculous; the best scores were so low the test should not have ever been given and the student learning of those topics was nil! However, that was used and recorded for final grading in the subject, implying satisfactory student learning. And the teacher moves on to new topics! The current argument justifying this type of grading process is that the questions are so hard the students are not expected to complete the test so the teacher is finding out the point their students reached in learning the overall material. This is very deceptive! What the teacher really should learn from the grading is the level of learning of the class, thereby documenting his/her teaching effectiveness of the topic objectives and what has to be done to improve learning. If the teacher's responsibility is student learning, then the teacher's responsibility has to be to ensure the learning of those not learning! *Tests really show how effective the teacher is relative to their student's learning.* Yes, many professional teachers will scoff at this, but if their paychecks were dependent upon how much information and how well their students learned, the professional attitude and teaching methods would improve overnight and many would be forced out of the profession. Right now, the overall learning of a class is camouflaged by only publishing individual grades to individual students. The real student learning effectiveness of the teacher is non-transparent and hidden in the class grade book. Let me share the following example of what I call "a curve grading disaster." This actually happened in a class I took. The course was related to applied mathematics and required the application of trigonometry to solve problems. The teacher would give weekly quizzes and selected five problems from numerous problems given at the end of each chapter in the course textbook. We, as a class of about 25 students, knew this and decided to meet at night, before the test, to work out the problems so everyone understood how to solve and show their work of the solutions. The teacher was a "curve grader" and extremely arrogant in that you were not allowed asking questions or receiving answers on homework during class. Therefore, we, the whole class, had an all-nighter working out the problems as a group until everyone really understood (learned) how to solve them. The next day we took the test, sure enough, the five questions were the ones from the text, and we received the results a few days afterward. This is educationally pathetic: The whole class received a grade of 100 percent, except for one person who had misplaced a decimal point—one decimal place, on one minor calculation, on one of the five questions. Because of that, and the grading on the curve process, he "failed" the test and was given an "F" for a grade even though the remainder of his test answers were all 100 percent correct. Think of this: We actually did the learning as a class ourselves out of desperation because of a very poor teacher who had no business in the classroom. In addition, the damage done to the student who received the "F" was distinct. I remember it as if it was yesterday. The student sat next to me, and I still remember the "perception" damage it did even though it was many years ago. Needless to say, the teacher was promoting "stay-outs," *and we were paying for it!* I cite this as an example of the differing perceived teacher responsibilities ranging from "preaching" to "student learning." Certainly this preacher's accepted job responsibility was to stand in front of the class we paid for and preach! In that case, he appeared he could have cared less about who was learning, who was not, and his effect on our perception of the education we were paying for. *This practice has to be eliminated from our educational system and the best place to start is in teacher education programs. Focus on student learning with the axiom, "The only failure in the classroom is the teacher."* Eliminate the curve grading process that seemingly justifies the awarding of A's through F's and teach to ensure learning to all in the class. That means teaching to ensure learning that produces a skewed curve resulting in more probable C's to A's.

Now, in the real world, we cannot expect every student will learn to expectations when we teach to "ensure learning," but logically learning would improve immeasurably over current methodologies and the perception of education would be less threatening, more inviting, and ultimately more effective.

A Thought

Why does the math class failure consistently understand and is able to apply complex odds at the racetrack? Why are computer science failures/dropouts interviewed and employed by major software manufacturers? Why does a science dropout make a major scientific breakthrough? Why are some of our most famous discoveries made by people not related to those specific fields? Why? Because, in the "Real World," necessity has consistently shown that it is the mother of invention. Therefore, teachers, convince students of a realistic necessity to learn that directly and positively interests them and they will ensure their learning in spite of you, not because of you!

Reform Teacher Education

- ▶ Learn how to create and document measurable objectives for all major topics within an academic course.
- ▶ Learn how to test and evaluate student learning (entirely eliminating curve grading) specifically related to course measurable objectives.
- ▶ Create learning experiences, for all disciplines, ethically utilizing all three modes of learning receptivity that effects the student to: "Remember it, remember how to do it, do it, and repeat it."

- Learn how to plan and implement teaching improvement by evaluating individual course measureable objectives versus corresponding class examination/test grades.
- Accept that the most important teaching job responsibility is "student learning."
- Display and develop a teaching commitment to the philosophy: "The only failure in the classroom is the teacher."

Chapter 7: Gender Bias

Teaching and Gender Bias

Unfortunately, "Gender Bias" exists in many forms in the home, the school, and the workplace. The problem, most importantly in schools, is that the results of gender bias influences the decisions students make in the coursework they take, which in turn influences, and ultimately may limit, their career choices. In reality, this influence is a serious career determining issue and the more we work to eliminate bias the more career opportunities we open to students, regardless of gender. As to the seeds of gender bias: I believe the shaping of knowledge of one's mind is like programming a computer, from birth and on. *We tend to learn what we live and we live what we learn.* Unfortunately, some of our positive intentions we do as parents, teachers, role models, etc. have unknowing, unrealistic and sometimes negative consequences. In this chapter, I will specifically focus on gender biases from home and in education and their effects. To this end, I will draw on my own experience, both as an educator and a parent.

To begin with, educational research indicates there are fewer women in math and science related disciplines specifically because of differences either in: socialization practices between men and women, the way math and science are taught in elementary and secondary education, traditional advisement in schools, and personal/family obligations. The fact is all of these factors appear to contribute to the under-representation of females in science related employment versus their male counterparts.

The socialization issue begins early in family life with different role expectations between boys and girls. Examples of expectations begin with boys whose expectations are, many times perceived and vocalized by their parents, to grow up to be in more masculine perceived occupations such as builders, tradesmen, engineers, sports players, etc. Whereas girls are many times perceived and vocalized to grow up to be in more "feminine perceived" occupations such as models, nurses, secretaries, elementary school teachers, or less masculine fields. These roles, too many times, are self-fulfilling in that we try to become what is expected of us.

Unfortunately, what is expected of us is too many times perceived from tradition rather than logical ability. What I mean is girls and boys have similar basic scholastic abilities yet are steered by biases and tradition rather than generated interest. Additional factors relating to the way gender is differentiated are often times related to geographical norms, religious beliefs, family economics, ethnic and racial backgrounds, etc. I believe all of these factors tend to promote unbalanced career choices resulting in too many students not becoming what they are capable of being, or really interested in being.

Now, going from the home front to school, the gender biases advance and increase seemingly unnoticed but in themselves are a very strong influence in academic course decision making, and thus subsequent career decisions. In education, gender bias tends to begin in the elementary school, continues to the secondary level, and so on. For the most part the coursework developed at these levels is not developed to engage female curiosity. Most lessons presented in the classroom are unknowingly gender biased as historical contributions made by women in science are not emphasized in the curriculum, versus their male counterparts, nor is the course material presented to accommodate the different learning styles of girls and women. The first educational barrier encountered by female students is the presentation of math and science curriculums. Research shows little bias in the early elementary years, but in middle school females begin to show a more negative attitude toward math and science than males.

In reality, females, in general, have fewer science experiences than males do. Males have a substantially greater history of working with or fixing something electrical/mechanical than females do. Overall, females are not exposed to toys and activities that ignite their curiosity about science and tend to be less exposed to science in general. This disinterest in science, and resultant math requirements leads females to avoid taking the advanced courses necessary for careers in science. When they graduate from high school, they are not academically equipped or motivated to pursue careers in science or engineering. Therefore, fewer females enroll in science-related programs after they finish high school.

It is logical that to lessen/eliminate gender bias in middle and high school curriculums the teachers need to address the interests and learning styles of women. Additionally, the contributions made by women have to be acknowledged in order to sustain female long-term interest. Herein, as most scientists are male, science traditionally has represented a male point of view. Teaching becomes less gender biased when classroom experimentation focuses more on concerns with social significance and less on specialized mechanical applications. Additionally, solving problems more traditionally female oriented and using less gender-biased language allows females to feel less alienated by the process. Examples used in the classroom such as the trajectory of a spacecraft or the mechanical workings of a car are gender biased and few females can relate to the subject matter from prior experience. Because females cannot readily relate to the material, they lose interest and gravitate toward subjects with which they feel more relevance.

Typical advisement in school has its own hidden biases. Studies of junior high school students show too many male and female students are unaware of career options available to them as well as their educational requirements. Much school advisement and career advisement is predicated on past grades and coursework and this is then used as an *inaccurate* predictor of future options and success. Thus, many are counseled into traditional career tracks rather than areas of genuine interest, which would necessitate problem solving with the student on how and what to do to achieve career interests and goals. As a former statistics professor once indicated, "National studies conducted to follow students from school to work in order to predict outcomes, based on hundreds of variables, could only reveal with confidence that boys could lift heavier weights than girls." "Any other variable relationships had little significance and were sheer speculation." After many years in the educational system, both as a teacher and administrator, I have to agree advisement based on past performance is time poorly spent. In fact, it is negative because it plants the seed "I can only become something based on what I have already done." This type of thinking has to be abolished in the real world of education and work. Note: people tend to do well what they want to do, and the converse also holds true.

Can you believe some schools still adhere to local and geographical advisement norms such as "boys take shop and girls take home economics?" I hope we have passed that form of thinking but it is a typical example of illogical and gender biased advisement. I have witnessed this practice, in not the too distant past, in very progressive school districts and watched it practiced by very educated people. Gender bias exists in such simple forms we really do not realize it until we look back and recognize the ignorance of it all. I actually know an example of a female student who had to get middle-school board approval to *not* take home economics, in order to take shop instead. The shop course consisted of one semester of mechanical drawing and one semester of hands-on producing what was drawn. It was a personal interest decision that defied local advisement norms and required the permission of the school board and its president. The student was just an average young student who had an interest in mechanical arts instead of home economics. She, after significant persistence, received permission only after getting a male student to agree to take her place in the home economics class. Both students had interests differing from advisement norms. This scenario occurred in a middle school and the female continued through the normal high school curriculum and then went on to college. I knew the female student and attended her college graduation where she received a degree in Mechanical Engineering. Her acceptance of advisement from her college coursework faculty consisted of how to solve the problems related to achieving one's goal, instead of her formal high school adviser's advisement that said: "Your math background is to insufficient in order compete in calculus so try a less demanding career." I like to believe the middle school "shop course" and her college faculty significantly influenced her career choice and resultant success.

Whether we realize it or not, most teachers themselves are advising students all the time by their perceived actions, statements, looks, demeanor, biases, etc. Teacher gender in itself is a perceived bias because there are significantly more men teaching in math and science at the college level and females feel in the minority for both support and true "peer" advisement. Classroom climate and a lack of role models all seem to have a negative impact on female science oriented students. At the college level, faculty are often required to conduct research and publish in addition to regular teaching duties, therefore females tend to choose a science-oriented career in industry because it is more "time compatible" with family life. That is, industrial companies are more likely to allow women to work part-time than at academic institutions. The absence of female faculty for peer support of female science oriented students is a severe detriment to attracting females into science-oriented curriculums.

CHAPTER 7: GENDER BIAS

Relative to this, on limited occasions, I have seen female students seek advisement and peer support from female faculty and, because of that relationship, remain in and successfully complete an academic program that I believe they would not have, had there been no female support.

As previously described, female students are less likely than men to choose a career in science due to a litany of reasons. Actually, females currently comprise approximately 20 percent of the science and engineering labor force in our country, but comprise approximately half the labor force in total. The reasons for this disproportion are certainly diverse but gender bias from home, to and including school, are major factors. So, teachers, just being a teacher has a strong gender impact on the perception of students and carries a professional responsibility to promote knowledge and career opportunities emphasizing gender equality. Again, the only failure to accomplish this in the classroom can be the teacher.

A THOUGHT

I remember an actual phone conversation involving an employee of a parts manufacturing company that was under contract to one of the big three U.S. automakers. The employee called the automaker plant and wanted to discuss an engineering problem they were having with the item they were producing for the plant. The employee transferred by phone tree to the engineering department of the automaker and a *female* voice answered with "Engineering Department, may I help you?" The employee, without hesitation, quickly responded with "I need to talk to an engineer." After a short pause, the *female* voice respectively responded, "I am an engineer." Another short pause and an UN-realizing apology.

REFORMS TO ELIMINATE GENDER BIAS IN EDUCATION

- Eliminate language in the classroom that promotes biased perceptions of occupations and successful people by relating to their specific gender.

- Reduce male gender biased examples used in problem explanations, solutions, and increase female related examples.

- Increase, earlier in education, career advisement that focuses on UN-biased gender career options and education requirements to achieve those options.

- Focus student advisement on what a student wants to do, and how they can do it, rather than what they are limited to because of past performance.

- Increase female teachers in science and mathematics; serving as both faculty, student mentors, and underrepresented role models.

- Promote female student organizations for traditionally male-dominated curriculums.

Chapter 8: Managing Teaching Improvement

The Processes

What is "Administration and Management?" Well, in practice, someone has to be the leader, the person responsible, or so to speak the manager. In education, we call it administration. Teachers, like most other employees, figuratively report to an administrator such as a Department Chair, Department Head, Vice Principle, etc. These positions are generally responsible for the day-to-day management of the faculty. That means being responsible for *faculty/staff hiring and* **evaluation,** *scheduling, meetings, professional development (training), department events, budgeting, etc.*

Evaluation: This is, without doubt, the most important responsibility of the faculty administrator. The evaluation process should document a faculty member's "student learning" effectiveness, and subsequent to that the preparation and implementation of a continuous teaching improvement plan, all subject to the faculty member's reappointment. *This, for the most part, is a non-existent process.*

A Logical Thought

A continuous faculty evaluation/improvement process, based specifically on the documented level of student learning versus corresponding topic objectives, reveals the effectiveness of a teacher's teaching. The results of this can be analyzed and improvements planned to increase future student learning. *This is generally known as the process of continuous improvement, though almost non-existent in education, is already well proven in the real world!* Again, the foremost job responsibility of the teacher should be student learning therefore a comprehensive student final examination, or cumulative test grades, should be used to compute a "class grade average" for each course the teacher teaches. This would clearly show faculty, administration, and the consumers how well the entire class of students learned the measurable objectives of the course and reveal the effectiveness of the teacher. Again, the documented level of student learning should be the most important criteria in faculty evaluation, along with the faulty member's plan for continuous improvement and their reappointment predicated on the performance of that plan. Ironically, some will say it already is! I say, if it really were, then all existing faculty would be considered adequately improving and or excellent; this is obviously not the case. How often have you heard or read a faculty member was released because of poor student learning resulting from poor teaching? Come on! Yes, some are released for committing a felony but, for the most part, I cannot ever remember any faculty member let go because of documented poor student learning. *Heck, there is not even a common system in place to document, evaluate, and improve a faulty member's teaching effectiveness based on their collective student's learning of topic/course objectives.*

It is common knowledge our national high school dropout rate is disastrous; the community colleges are filled with students who had poor preparatory learning in high school accompanied by an additional number of prior student "stay-outs" who vowed never to return! However, some teachers remain in their jobs under the premise that acceptable (undocumented) learning takes place. This is an absurd premise! It is almost amusing listening to the statement by some faculty who expound to others they have 20 or so years of experience, implying they are an excellent teacher. In reality, what we have is a teacher with one-year of experience *(not evaluated by how well the students learned the topics he/she was responsible for)* and most often repeated for the next 19 years. I can only say this is the problem, not the solution, and is the breeding ground for an accelerated dropout and stay-out education system. The faculty administrator must be responsible for requiring all faculty to have clearly written measurable course objectives and a comprehensive final examination or cumulative tests to assess student learning of the course objectives. This should be reviewed and approved by the faculty administrator before the course begins, monitored at specified intervals, and then ultimately utilized to compute the "class grade average," thus documenting the teacher's effectiveness.

FINAL EXAMINATIONS

It is generally accepted final examinations occur at the end of a course of study and the elementary and secondary school systems (responsibility of the state) regularly promote various configurations of that requirement. It is also generally accepted this is not always the case at the post-secondary or college level. I am aware many courses of study at the college level forgo a final examination, growing numbers to the extent that at least one regional accreditation commission now requires a "culminating experience" at the end of the course. This appears to be language that requires something to happen at the end of the course, promotes faulty flexibility in decision making, and is many times construed by faculty to mean anything from a class get-together, informal class question/answer debate, or the likes. Herein lies the problem: In order to document the effectiveness of the teaching we have to determine the level of learning of the students. A most logical and ethical way is to have a comprehensive examination at the end of each course, which is based on the measurable objectives of the course. How can we improve if we do not know what we have done? In short, it should be required of all public learning institutions that comprehensive final examinations or cumulative interval tests (based on all course measureable objectives) occur for all students enrolled in a course. No student exceptions, no exemptions, etc.

The implementation of this process must be the responsibility of the faculty administrator. It is the very foundation of continuous improvement, both for the teacher and the students. Be aware that improvement in education, or any organization, does not just happen. It is developed through a continuous process of improvement until the organization reaches the point its performance is publicly recognized to be better than anyone else does, and it becomes the leader by recognition. Without continuous improvement the contrary occurs!

CHAPTER 8: MANAGING TEACHING IMPROVEMENT

CURRENT FACULTY EVALUATION

Unfortunately, the most common faculty evaluation process I have witnessed rarely looks at the student grade picture derived from final examinations or any other student testing for that matter. Why? Many courses do not have clearly written and measurable topic objectives. Those courses preached from a textbook can utilize the text chapter objectives, but a course final examination or cumulative tests should be developed to comprehensively measure the student achievement of those objectives, and to determine the effectiveness of the teaching. Where there are few written and measurable objectives it is next to impossible to clearly identify student learning, and the level of learning of those objectives. Therefore, what might be reviewed are the final course grades from the final course grade sheets submitted by the teacher. This hardly indicates the level of student learning of specific course objectives unless the teacher has the evaluation instruments (the tests) tied to each course objective. There are instances where teachers might practice this process but, for the most part, the final grades reflect accumulated quizzes, documents, rewards, and the results of a generalized final test, if it is given at all. The major problem is teachers are not evaluated critically on the learning level of their students because, in too many cases, there are no measurable objectives tied to evaluative tests for the topics the teacher is teaching. *I found this situation to be more prevalent at the college level.* Even if there were credible tests for the subjects the teacher is teaching, the reappointment of the teacher by administration would and could not be determined on that data. Why? Because faculty evaluation is generally so skewed by other evaluative factors that student learning, if documented at all, would only be a small fractional part of the overall review. Again, where or when have you heard of a faculty member being released because of poor student learning? Whom is it failing? The students of course, as well as the taxpayers, parents, and others who are paying the bill for that system. Unfortunately, the system is so ingrained in a teacher evaluation process that ultimately protects poor faculty performance and successfully resists attempts to replace them by administrators. Had faculty member's been contractually responsible for student learning and the standardized test or other test results tied to comprehensive measurable objectives revealed student learning was at an unacceptable level, the administration would at least have documentation to support necessary improvement or non-reappointment. In too many examples a faculty member has continuing reappointment because of tenure, is not contractually responsible for student learning, and the school system, given the legal roadblocks, would not even attempt removal. Therefore, poor teaching continues, students drop out, and we wonder why our schools have the problems they do, so we legislate more money into the system (new curriculum concepts) and wind up with the same result. That is why legislating more money into a broken system will not work. The current public educational system needs overhaul renovation, or "reform" to function in the real world. From my experience our current public educational system; for the most part, though not all, illogically protects poor teaching that results in poor student learning. This is just the opposite of what we as reasonable parents, taxpayers, educational leaders, or interested people want. To have accountability in the teaching system we must hold teachers accountable for their job responsibility, specifically "to impart knowledge." Then, measure their effectiveness by documenting and analyzing the "imparting of knowledge;" *the student learning that took place.* Based on that analysis, make changes to improve future student learning and continue the process as the major part of a faculty member's annual evaluation. This, I believe, will be a resisted concept because it is threatening to so many. Ironically, I know a few teachers, who would welcome it, do not see it as a threat, because their teaching goal is "student learning." If their students were not learning, the way they wanted them to, they would make immediate changes in order to have their students learn. Anything less would be an insult to their ability. They are *the few, the proud,* and are far between in a system that resultantly functions to support and even promote poor teaching performance. I readily admit many in the current system do not support the processes of the system; they see the resultant failings of such a system, but are trapped by rules and negotiated contractual terms appearing too demonstrable to change.

IMPORTANT CONCEPTS

Begin with accepting the concept the most important person in the classroom is the student—what they learn, and at what level they learn. Most will acknowledge the student is the most important person, but the real issue will be "at what level they learn." This will be resisted with the current teacher argument, "I have no control of their level of learning," "I teach and it is up to them as individuals to learn." This argument leads to teacher complacency, apathy, and is the major problem we face, not the solution. The good teachers have the common goal of student learning as their main purpose in the classroom. Not because someone told them to, but because they believe it is their professional responsibility as a teacher. This seems to be the common value of those teachers who receive awards for excellent teaching. So then, what and at what level, the students learn should be the primary concern of everyone. That primary concern must be the primary responsibility of the employed teacher. Being the primary responsibility, the teacher should be evaluated on their student's documented level of learning. In addition, the reappointment of teachers should be primarily based on their student's documented level of learning. To do this, many current accepted practices will have to change. This will not be easy. Documented measurable topic objectives in all courses, comprehensive testing of the objectives to document student learning, and teacher evaluation and reappointment based on the level of student learning that took place and a process of continuous improvement.

Contrary to the advocates of the current system, we do not have measurable topic objectives in all courses, we do not have testing of those objectives (some yes but far from all), and certainly teacher evaluation and reappointment *is not* based on a documented level of student learning. This concept of documenting student learning does not take away the freedom of the curriculum designers or specialty offerings of differing schools, it only holds the teachers, administration, and schools accountable for student learning.

If we are paying dollars for teacher's salaries, and we make the effort to go to school, we want to be confident we are going to learn! In the "real world," this is more than reasonable and just makes sense. Everything else prior to this is just advertised lip service and has put the burden of the production of the product on the consumer, the student, instead of the product producer, the school and teacher. Unbelievable that common sense logic evolved years ago from "pay for what you get—or learn" to public education's now "pay for a teacher in spite of what you get or learn" and deftly persists in our "business oriented" society. This has to reverse itself in order for the United States to become a real world leader in education.

A THOUGHT

The most important question schools should answer about student learning is: What is the minimum acceptable level of student learning as determined by a comprehensive final examination or cumulative testing "class grade average" for classes taught at the institution? How is it determined, documented, made public, and then analyzed in the faculty reappointment process.

Now, how often or, when have you ever seen the total spread of final examination grades for an entire class? Forget about student names, just the final examination grades or cumulative test grades for all students in the class and, collectively, how that depicts the overall level of learning taking place in the class? Never published, never talked about, never, whatever! It is time the public bill payers require schools to publish their teacher's effectiveness for individual classes so the taxpayers and potential students see what they are getting for their money. Yes, the taxpayers are actually paying the salaries of the public school's faculty, staff, and administrators even though the dollars go through a convoluted evolution of fiscal dispersal. What difference do you think it would make if you had to hand the actual wage money to the faculty, staff, and administrators (all in person) after the course was completed? I think the institutions would respond more positively to personal financial confrontation and/or reimbursement and become less defensive and more "amenably motivated" for lack of a better term. Because this will probably not occur in our complex system, we must have a built in mandate of "continuous improvement" (as previously described) to counter complacency and its various viruses, enabling education to function in the real world where strong performance and value predicts success.

Reform the Management of Teachers

- Document and make publicly available all faculty member's class grade averages and resultant levels of teaching effectiveness (derived by final examinations or cumulative tests) for the most recent classes taught.
- Determine the learning institution's minimally acceptable "class grade average" for student learning and teaching effectiveness.
- Ensure all faculty, for all courses, have clearly written measureable objectives for all major course topics and comprehensive final examinations or cumulative tests assessing student learning of those objectives.
- Ensure comprehensive final examinations or cumulative tests take place for all classes and a subsequent "class grade average" is documented, to grade the level

of student learning and resultant teaching effectiveness.

- Ensure all faculty, for every contract period, *at least annually,* prepare an acceptable continuous teaching improvement plan evaluating individual course measureable objectives versus corresponding class examination/test grades.

- Ensure that all faculty re-appointment contracts are subject to attaining an acceptable level of teaching effectiveness (class grade average) and a continuous improvement teaching plan.

Chapter 9: Ethics and Teaching

Responsibilities

In the Real World "Ethics" are perceived as practicing good conduct and having moral principles or values. More accurately the dictionary defines it as the "rules or standards governing the conduct of members of a profession." This definitely relates to the teaching profession and thus directly affects student learning. Remember, we learn what we live and thus we live what we learned. The effect that a teacher's ethics has on the perceptions learned by students is prolific. One only has to read and study the written student evaluations of faculty to realize the profound affect the values of the teacher has on the perception of the students. There are few classes that I personally have taken where the teacher's political views and other personal values have not been forthcoming. Some to the outright extent that it could clearly affect one's relationship with the teacher and subsequently one's perception of the grade they received. Faculty projection of personal/political views is a breeding ground for deceptive learning and must be eliminated from the learning environment.

It is well accepted in the education profession that the teacher is the leader in the classroom and must conduct themselves at the highest level of perceived values. Remember students are learning from the teacher's perceived actions as well as their words. Personal views and actions relating to religion, politics, morality, and other controversially potential subjects should be avoided unless they are an integral part of the course being taught. Where controversial subjects are a required part of the course, and discussed, it is the teacher's responsibility to present both sides of the issue with the intent of providing enough non-biased information so students can make their own judgement decisions in a non-biased atmosphere.

In practice it appears that "ethics" seems to be a subject in teaching practice and evaluation that is generally avoided until a problem occurs and then pundits refer to the obvious "ethical professional responsibility" of the person or whatever in question; after the fact. I was aware of strong discussion within at least one regional accreditation commission that "ethics" should be a required course in all professional programs but that gained little support because it would require lengthening the program of study which is not a popular topic. The substitute to an actual new course was the accepted notion that "ethics" it is a subject already "embedded" in the curriculum. This meant that the teacher discusses ethics as the need arises within the various courses of the curriculum. My experience is that this does not appear to happen as suggested and is nothing more than verbal dissent against logical improvement;

even in light of significant numbers of teacher violations relating to ethical conduct. Just read the continual media reports of public teachers being involved in conduct contrary to their professional responsibilities. This type of non-ethical behavior has no place in education because it is the teacher's professional responsibility to *always* set a positive example of character and values.

The following description just about sums up "ethics" in education. A teacher must be both a manager and a leader. The manager of the classroom environment and the leader of the group and subject being taught. The ethical responsibilities of both positions are well defined by the paraphrase: "Managers must do things right—Leaders must do the right things."

Chapter 10: Reforms for Schools and Colleges

To: Parents, Students, Educators, Lawmakers, and the General Public:

Question: What type of school would you choose? One that tells you what you are going to learn, how you are going to learn it, and the effectiveness of the teacher; all before you pay? Or, the "current contrary!" Choice can be a reality when schools adopt and implement the following reforms:

Reform Current Teaching and Learning (Chapter 1)

- Teachers and administrators must directly accept responsibility and accountability (be answerable) for student learning.
- Limit selective teaching by "preaching" (expounding, lecture—telling).
- Teach by ethically utilizing all three modes of learning receptivity for all course objectives.

- Develop student interest in all the subjects taught in the classroom.
- Promote student accomplishment for all students in the classroom.
- Measure, grade, and analyze student learning thus documenting teacher effectiveness.

Reforms to Teach More Effectively (Chapter 2)

- Accept personal and professional responsibility for student learning.
- Inspire student motivation and generate a cause to learn for all course topics.
- Create measureable objectives for all major course topics.
- Teach by ethically utilizing all three modes of learning receptivity for all course objectives.
- Document a "class grade average," grading the level of learning of all course measureable objectives and resultant teaching effectiveness, for each assigned course.
- Compute the "class grade average," using comprehensive final examination grades or cumulative test grades; all enrolled students—no exemptions.
- Prepare a continuous teaching improvement plan; evaluating individual course measureable objectives versus corresponding class examination/test grades.

Chapter 10: Reforms for Schools and Colleges

Reforms to Ensure Learning (Chapter 3)

- Ethically incorporate all three receptive learning modes for teaching all course measurable objectives.
- Create genuine student interest in all course objectives and abolish threats of failure or threats of any kind.
- Create intermittent course tests to measure student learning and evaluate teaching effectiveness of all major course objectives. Utilize the results for the improvement of instruction, such as re-teaching, versus student grading.
- Display a recognizable classroom attitude and demeanor that the teacher's primary priority is "student learning."

Reform Teacher Evaluation (Chapter 4)

- Document measurable course objectives for all major course topics taught.
- Document comprehensive final examinations and cumulative tests that include all major course measurable objectives, for all courses taught.
- Document a "class grade average for each assigned course, grading the class level of learning and resultant teaching effectiveness.
- Compute the "class grade average" using the comprehensive final examination grades or cumulative test grades: all enrolled students, no exemptions.
- Prepare a continuous teaching improvement plan; evaluating individual course measureable objectives versus corresponding class examination/test grades.

- Demonstrate re-appointment based on acceptable class grade averages in the most recent classes, and an acceptable continuous teaching improvement plan.

Reform Teacher Contracts (Chapter 5)

- Identify all courses the teacher is assigned to teach.
- Require preparation of measurable objectives for all major topics in each course assigned.
- Require comprehensive final course examinations that include all major course measurable objectives, for all students enrolled in all courses assigned, no exemptions.
- Document a "class grade average," grading the level of learning of all course measureable objectives and resultant teaching effectiveness, for each assigned course.
- Compute the "class grade average," using comprehensive final examination grades or cumulative test grades; all enrolled students, no exemptions.
- Demonstrate an acceptable level of teaching effectiveness based on the most recent "class grade averages."
- Prepare a continuous improvement teaching plan; evaluating individual course measureable objectives versus corresponding class examination/test grades.
- Receive, for contract reappointment, approval of all aforementioned requirements.

Reform Teacher Education (Chapter 6)

- Learn how to create and document measurable objectives for all major topics within an academic course.
- Learn how to test and evaluate student learning (entirely

Chapter 10: Reforms for Schools and Colleges

eliminating curve grading) specifically related to course measurable objectives.

- Create learning experiences, ethically utilizing all three modes of learning receptivity for all disciplines, that effects the student to: "Remember it, remember how to do it, do it, and repeat it."
- Learn how to generate continuous teaching improvement by evaluating individual course measureable objectives versus corresponding class examination/test grades.
- Accept that the most important teaching job responsibility is "student learning."
- Display and develop a teaching commitment to the philosophy: "The only failure in the classroom is the teacher."

Reforms to Eliminate Gender Bias in Education (Chapter 7)

- Eliminate language in the classroom that promotes biased perceptions of occupations and successful people by relating to their specific gender.
- Reduce male gender biased examples used in problem explanation and solutions, and increase female related examples.
- Increase, earlier in education, career advisement that focuses on UN-biased gender career options and education requirements to achieve those options.
- Focus student advisement on what a student wants to do, and how they can do it, rather than what they are limited to because of past performance.
- Increase female teachers in science and mathematics,

serving as faculty, student mentors, and under-represented role models.

- Promote female student organizations for traditionally male-dominated curriculums.

Reform the Management of Teachers (Chapter 8)

- Document and make publicly available all faculty member's class grade averages and resultant levels of teaching effectiveness (derived by final examinations or cumulative tests) for the most recent classes taught.

- Determine the learning institution's minimally acceptable "class grade average" for student learning and teaching effectiveness.

- Ensure all faculty, for all courses, have clearly written measureable objectives for all major course topics and comprehensive final examinations or cumulative tests assessing student learning of those objectives.

- Ensure comprehensive final examinations or cumulative tests take place for all classes and a subsequent "class grade average" is documented, to grade the level of student learning and resultant teaching effectiveness.

- Ensure all faculty, for every contract period, *at least annually,* prepare an acceptable continuous teaching improvement plan evaluating individual course measureable objectives versus corresponding class examination/test grades.

- Ensure that all faculty re-appointment contracts are subject to attaining an acceptable level of teaching effectiveness (class grade average) and a continuous improvement teaching plan.

CHAPTER 10: REFORMS FOR SCHOOLS AND COLLEGES

A FINAL THOUGHT

The Beginning of this Story for me started in the "Real World" because, in the real world, experience has demonstrated shifting the responsibility for the performance of a product, to the creator of the product, positively increases the product's performance. *Do we really have to wonder why?* Now, imagine an auto producer who did not have to be responsible for the cars they produce. We probably would be driving low quality, high emissions, and vehicles that are more dangerous compared to the current vehicles; the responsibility for which is held accountable by purchasers, consumer groups, numerous related agencies, and courts of law. What is probably just as notorious as a non-accountable product producer is a publicly funded education system that is not specifically accountable for the most important product it produces, "student learning." It could, and does, represent a system that can flounder in any direction because in the "real world" continuous review, analysis, and improvement are most logically derived from and applied to the product produced. In education; continuous review, analysis, and improvement are inconsequential because they are not derived from and applied to documented "student learning." One of my former colleagues once characterized the operations of such a system as "a dice shoot aboard the deck of an aircraft carrier in a typhoon." Ironically, if we have survived this long without documenting and analyzing student learning, *specifically for the sake of continuous improvement,* think of what we would be able to do with an educational system committed to the aforementioned "reforms."

In any established organization, a change, or more particularly a reform, is "a hard pill to swallow." We have been doing it this way for years and it has worked out O.K., why change now? So look around readers! Is what you see the same as yesteryear? In current times concepts, products, media, and the human response to change evolves so fast it is hard to keep abreast of even the language that accompanies the change. The reality is, if we do not move with it, those in the business of public education will be in the business of going out of business. The invitation to, and the attractiveness of, proprietary education in our country, in just the last few years, has been phenomenal. It is too easy to feel job-protected when you are employed by a characteristically "slow to respond" protective giant institution like a city, county, or state. But, when the public seriously begins to question the producers of the educational product, because there are obvious problems with the product (mediocre ranking, drop-outs, stay-outs, low SAT scores etc.), the producers can only remain unresponsive and protected so long. Their rhetoric will no longer be able to resist the inquiry representing questions of, and demands for, *accountability*. Leaders who commit to "Reforming Education for the Real World" will be the reformers who specifically want the best education we can provide for *"all"* of our students. Unfortunately, promoting new concepts, curriculums, and programs in our system is an annual political never-ending debate of proposed solutions to our educational woes. However, in spite of those perpetual politically motivated endeavors *significant improvement in "student learning" is not forthcoming!* For the United States to be a world leader in education, educators must take the reformation lead in being accountable for their major job responsibility of "student learning."

That includes being answerable for the documented level of their students' learning and a subsequent process of continuous improvement. This is the most important step in "Reforming Education for the Real World!" Everything after that, reforms acknowledged herein, are merely the necessary *"academic"* steps.

That's the End of the Story

www.ingramcontent.com/pod-product-compliance
Lightning Source LLC
Chambersburg PA
CBHW021130300426
44113CB00006B/372